Praise for
Seven Keys to Unlock Autism

"Thank you, Elaine and Diane! *Seven Keys to Unlock Autism* is extraordinarily rich in wisdom and honest, practical advice. Welcome this book into your home and you will be inspired. Miracles are never easy, but they are closer than you think."
— Harvey Karp, MD, FAAP, creator of the DVD and book
The Happiest Toddler on the Block

"Elaine Hall's Miracle Project is a 'miracle'—a miracle of ingenuity, human intimacy, and creativity. This magnificent work vividly demonstrates the joy and hope of discovering the creative and emotional capacities that exist in all children but especially in those children with autism and other special needs."
— Stanley I. Greenspan, MD, author, *Engaging Autism* and
The Child with Special Needs

"What a remarkable guide for educators and care providers of people with ASD! In *Seven Keys to Unlock Autism*, Elaine Hall and Diane Isaacs urge us to live the timeless advice shared by Gandhi: 'You must be the change you want to see in the world.' In highly readable, engaging, and practical ways, Elaine and Diane challenge professionals and care providers to deeply explore places that few approaches to autism dare to go: how can we change OUR attitudes, beliefs, and actions to profoundly impact the lives of people with ASD in the most positive ways. This book is a rare work that is creative, optimistic, and deeply reflective. It will prove to be transformational for those of us who share their lives with people with ASD."
— Barry M. Prizant, PhD, CCC-SLP, director, Childhood
Communication Services, adjunct professor, Center for the
Study of Human Development, Brown University, and coauthor
of *The SCERTS Model*

"*Seven Keys to Unlock Autism* summarizes what we know about kids on the spectrum and how best to help them learn and thrive, in a concise yet warm and empathetic way. This book will prove to be extremely valuable to all members of the teaching community—as well as a child's lifelong teacher—his or her parent."
—Kristen Stills, Emmy-winning producer, *Autism: The Musical*, wife of Stephen Stills, mother, advocate

"This unique approach seamlessly blends the depth of the human spirit with an understanding of the neuroscience of autism. The Seven Keys help teachers and families to embrace children with differences and, ultimately, develop the opportunities, interactions, and expressive inner life we desire for all children. A must-read."
—CarolAnn Edscorn, MS, parent, advocate, educator

"Diane and Elaine packed *Seven Keys to Unlock Autism* full of great information for parents and professionals. I love that it comes with a bonus DVD for visual learners like me."
—Alex Plank, founder of WrongPlanet.net

"*Seven Keys to Unlock Autism* is an excellent resource for any professional working with students with autism. For new teachers it is a step-by-step guide that will help minimize anxiety and provide the framework for success in the classroom. For those of us in the field for a while, it is a refreshing new perspective that excites, motivates, and challenges us to recognize and develop these special individuals' strengths by increasing awareness of ourselves and the roadblocks we may unknowingly impose. Thankfully, Elaine and Diane help us know when to step out of the way and how to recognize, coach, and support these individuals' strengths."
—Debra Gordon, MS, CCC-SLP

"As children are diagnosed on the autism spectrum at ever increasing rates, *Seven Keys to Unlock Autism* is a must-read for mental health clinicians, educators, and others working with families. Anyone working with families touched by autism would be well equipped with the compassionate and commonsense approaches offered in this book."
—Ilene Weingarten, MFT

Seven Keys to Unlock Autism

Seven Keys to Unlock Autism

Making Miracles in the Classroom

Elaine Hall and Diane Isaacs

Foreword by Stephen M. Shore

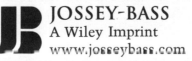

JOSSEY-BASS
A Wiley Imprint
www.josseybass.com

Published by Jossey-Bass
A Wiley Imprint
989 Market Street, San Francisco, CA 94103-1741—www.josseybass.com

Jossey-Bass books and products are available through most bookstores. To contact Jossey-Bass directly call our Customer Care Department within the U.S. at 800-956-7739, outside the U.S. at 317-572-3986, or fax 317-572-4002.

Wiley also publishes its books in a variety of electronic formats and by print-on-demand. Some material included with standard print versions of this book may not be included in e-books or in print-on-demand. If the version of this book that you purchased references media such as CD or DVD that was not included in your purchase, you may download this material at http://booksupport.wiley.com. For more information about Wiley products, visit www.wiley.com.

Library of Congress Cataloging-in-Publication Data
Hall, Elaine, date.
  Seven keys to unlock autism : making miracles in the classroom / Elaine Hall and Diane Isaacs ; foreword by Stephen M. Shore.
      p. cm.
  Includes bibliographical references and index.
  ISBN 978-0-470-64409-6 (cloth); ISBN 978-1-118-10267-1 (ebk.); ISBN 978-1-118-10268-8 (ebk.); ISBN 978-1-118-10269-5 (ebk.)
    1. Autistic children–Education–United States.   2. Autistic youth– Education–United States.   3. Inclusive education–United States.
I. Isaacs, Diane, date.   II. Title.
  LC4718.H35 2012
  371.94'044–dc23

                                                              2011022599

Printed in the United States of America
FIRST EDITION
HB Printing   10 9 8 7 6 5 4 3 2 1

Contents

*To our inspiring messengers, Wyatt and Neal,
who make miracles out of autism . . . every day*

Acknowledgments

A special spotlight shines on Marjorie McAneny for championing the seven keys when it was just a contender. Thank you to Irene Webb for her diligent and caring leadership and Tracy Columbus for her boundless energy and dedication to our mission.

Our special thanks to Elizabeth Kaye for her laser focus, Alisa Jones for her witty encouragement, Paula Stacey for her useful suggestions, and Lisa Johnson for her inspiration in and out of the trenches. And thanks to the brilliant experts in autism who have become our family: Stephen Shore, Barry Prizant, Dr. Ricki Robinson, DanaKae Bonahoom, and in loving memory of Dr. Stanley Greenspan.

Thank you to all of Neal's teachers and our experiences with them, which shaped Neal's educational program, especially to Miriam Brock, Darlene Hanson, Portia Iverson, Darci Kelleher, Wendy Parise, Mark Sanchegrin, Sarita Santos; and all of Neal's coaches, past and current. A heartfelt shout-out to the creative teachers we've encountered along Wyatt's wondrous path: Dawn Spagna, Jackie Sidman, Carol Ishihara, and the many artists of education at The Help Group.

To the imaginative Miracle Project kids, who clearly threw away the molds, and our expanding global network of Miracle Project practitioners, volunteers, and family members who lead autism forward with acceptance and joy. Thank you to everyone involved in The Vista Inspire Program at Vista Del Mar for your support of innovative autism programming.

Diane is in loving gratitude of her two sons, Jackson and Wyatt, who teach her by example to live in the now, transcend all limits, and be a dedicated ambassador of truth.

Elaine thanks her son, Neal, for teaching her to listen profoundly and know unconditional love. His courage and tenacity inspires her daily. She thanks her husband, play therapist Jeff Frymer, for "holding down the fort," cooking amazing meals, and being a wonderful husband and role model for Neal.

To all of us who have hit walls, found impassable obstacles, wanted to give up . . . but didn't. For you.

About the Authors

Elaine Hall ("CoachE!") was a top Hollywood children's acting coach working for Disney Studios, Universal Pictures, Nickelodeon, and others, including the film *Akeelah and the Bee.* Elaine's life changed dramatically after her son, Neal, adopted from a Russian orphanage, was diagnosed with autism. When traditional therapies did not work for him, she rallied actors and other cre-ative people to join his world, and Neal slowly emerged from his isolation. She then developed the Seven Keys training program and used these methods to create The Miracle Project, a world-renowned theater and film program for children of all abilities, profiled in the Emmy Award–winning HBO documentary *Autism: The Musical.*

Elaine has appeared on CNN, *CBS News,* Oprah Radio, and has been featured in the *Los Angeles Times,* the *New York Times,* the *Boston Globe,* and the *Wall Street Journal.* She has received awards from Holly Robinson Peete's HollyRod Foundation, Autism Speaks, Autism Society of Los Angeles, Senator Fran Pavley, the mayor of Los Angeles, Areva Martin's Special Needs Network, Etta Israel, and many more. Her innovative approach to working with children with autism has created a "movement," with people requesting The Miracle Project all over the world. Workshops have been held across the United States and Canada and in India and Africa. The Miracle Project now has ongoing classes in New York City, West Los Angeles, and at The Help Group in Los Angeles.

Elaine is a keynote speaker and workshop leader at conferences throughout the United States and Canada. Her first book, *Now I See the Moon: A Mother, a Son, a Miracle,* was chosen by the United Nations, where she spoke to launch World Autism Awareness Month 2011. Elaine and producer Diane Isaacs created the CD

Fly: Into Autism, which pairs kids with autism and celebrity artists and was honored at Carnegie Hall. In addition to her work with The Miracle Project, Elaine created and directs an arts enrichment program and a bar/bat mitzvah program for children and teens with autism at Vista Del Mar in Los Angeles. She lives in Santa Monica, California, with the two loves of her life, her teenage son, Neal, and her newly wedded play therapist husband, Jeff.

Photo: Cindy Gold

Diane Isaacs is an award-winning producer of film, television, and music. After she received her BFA in film and BA in English from New York University, she worked as an associate producer on *Miami Vice* and founded Green Moon Productions with Antonio Banderas and Melanie Griffith. She produced many films, including HBO's Emmy-nominated *And Starring Pancho Villa as Himself*, and worked with talented actors such as Academy Award–winners Emma Thompson and Helen Hunt, Patrick Swayze, Betty White, Mischa Barton, and Rod Steiger. She produced The Miracle Project benefit CD *Fly* with celebrity artists who performed duets with children with autism and directed The Miracle Project Fly Singers' YouTube hit *Sensitive* with Jack Black, the grand prize music video winner for Stand Up To Cancer, as well as the DVD series *Unlocking the World of Autism*.

A conference presenter and workshop leader, Diane has taught The Miracle Project and the Seven Keys nationally and internationally, including in India and Africa. Diane is an all-American, world-class Ironman athlete, achieving fourth place at the world championships in Kona, Hawaii, in 2004. Featured in *Sports Illustrated* and *Muscle & Fitness Hers*, she has developed Miracles 360, a mind, body, and spirit approach to fitness and wellness. She is a mother of two inspiring sons: Jackson, who gracefully balances competitive tennis, academics, and global inquiry, and Wyatt, who reminds her daily that "autism is awesomism!"

About The Miracle Project

Elaine Hall founded The Miracle Project in 2004. This transformational program had a simple yet visionary goal: to provide a loving, accepting, nurturing environment that celebrates and honors the unique and often unrecognized abilities of young people with autism and address other special needs by guiding them through creative workshops and artistic programs. In 2006, a documentary film, *Autism: The Musical*, was made that featured The Miracle Project and its methods. In 2007, *Autism: The Musical* premiered to rave reviews at the Tribeca Film Festival and was shown on HBO in April 2008, garnering two Emmy awards. Today, The Miracle Project is internationally acclaimed and uplifts thousands of children with autism.

To achieve this result, Elaine developed a specific, seven-pronged training program for her staff that consisted of educators, therapists, theater professionals, and carefully selected volunteers. Most had no previous experience in working with children with autism. The benefits of this training were clear to see. By learning to connect with the children and accept them for who they were, each trainee created relationships that infused the children with joy, confidence, and love. The trainees also bloomed as their newfound relationships increased their senses of empathy and compassion and brought them meaning and fulfillment.

Diane Isaacs, an accomplished television and film producer, experienced the benefits of The Miracle Project firsthand. As she traveled coast to coast and around the world, from Africa to Asia, she saw the pressing need for effective personal tools for those living and working with autism. She became determined to disseminate the inspiring Miracle Project's protocols using her multimedia experience. She joined forces with Elaine to bring you the *Seven Keys to Unlock Autism*.

How do Diane and Elaine know that the seven keys work? Because they have trained hundreds of people who started out with little or no knowledge of how to work with children with autism and were, through this program, immediately able to interact with them and understand them. The seasoned professionals trained in these protocols uniformly assert that they learned more about relating to children with autism through the seven keys than they learned in twenty previous years of teaching.

This book is designed to bring the seven keys to educators. Elaine and Diane recruited Lisa Johnson, a special education pioneer, and other special educators to provide hands-on teaching experience. They also enlisted those whose voices are rarely heard: students and teachers who have autism.

One of the great things about the seven keys is those who implement them have discovered that enlivening transformation occurs in the lives of their students and in their own lives.

We work in order to help others but also we help others in order to work on ourselves.
Pema Chödrön, Buddhist philosopher

Foreword

When the teacher is ready, the student will appear.

These were the first words that came to mind as I talked with Elaine Hall and Diane Isaacs about their book, *Seven Keys to Unlock Autism*. Borrowing from the ancient wisdom of Buddhist philosophy, which holds that students need to first be open to new ideas, thoughts, and experiences before truly learning, this book is about how teachers can open themselves up in both mind and heart to their students on the autism spectrum.

Beginning with a refreshing look at the autism spectrum, Elaine and Diane reframe kids with autism as simply different, rather than disordered. Certainly there are many aspects of autism that can be disordering, and we are duty-bound to provide support and intervention in these areas. However, the goal of intervention should be to help people with autism achieve as fulfilling and productive lives as possible with their differences—not in spite of, or in an effort toward, elimination of this condition.

Suppose a teacher has just been informed that a child with autism is joining her classroom. Typically, a deficit model would be employed—the bulk of the teacher's preparation would be accounting for and focusing on the challenges the student. However, if the student were introduced as an individual with significant strengths in visual processing and logic or has an unusual talent for vocal imitation, imagine how the educator's intentions, expectations, and preparations change. This book provides the tools for teachers to appreciate children as the individuals they are, recognize their strengths, and pave the way for building productive relationships so each and every student can receive the rich education that he and she deserves.

Like a polished diamond, this brilliant book educates readers in seven vital ways to open up to what students on the spectrum have to offer us in terms of personal growth and pedagogy. This guide is chock-full of wisdom and exercises that can be implemented today—activities that are profound in their simplicity and their effectiveness, such as the idea of "rebooting the day" to start afresh as needed, at any time, to bring in positivity. These seven essential keys unlock for readers a greater awareness, acceptance, and appreciation of the gifts waiting to be reaped from relationships with people having the fascinating, sometimes vexing (but rewarding in the end), condition we call autism.

This must-read guide is a powerful resource for parents, therapists, educators at all levels of experience, and others who want to learn more about supporting people with autism: appreciating and understanding who they are while simultaneously unlocking the keys for greater fulfillment on the part of all involved.

The seven keys prepare readers for successful relationships with people on the autism spectrum. Only when the teacher is ready—when an educator is open to accepting and appreciating students with autism as they are—will the student appear, ready to engage in miraculous personal growth, and to make the world a better place for all.

August 2011   Stephen M. Shore, EdD
Assistant professor of special education, Adelphi University
Internationally known consultant, presenter, and author
Person on the autism spectrum

Introduction

It Starts with You

I t's the start of a new school year. You've been handed your roster. Jonas Redden is in your class. Your first thoughts are, "What am I going to do? I've seen Jonas through the years. He can't sit down in class; he gets up out of his seat unexpectedly, spins in circles, and blurts out inappropriate sounds. He goes everywhere with a one-on-one aide and a talking machine."

You tell the principal that you're worried about how a student like Jonas might disrupt the class. You don't mention the fact that you've never received training in working with kids with autism! The principal says you have no choice. Like it or not, Jonas is going to be part of your class.

You wonder, "How can I possibly be successful with Jonas?" You may even feel sorry for yourself and ask, "Why me?"

Why you? Because, with an open mind, an open heart, and some understanding of autism, you will find that a boy like Jonas can be *your* greatest teacher. Jonas and his autism may open doors to your own inner world and teach you more than any student you have ever taught.

"But how do I *work* with him?" you ask. Nothing in your education has given you any clues about working with a child who has severe challenges. If you are like many teachers, there is little or no support from the administration. They, too, are overworked and juggling too many balls. Dollars are tight. The few basic interventions you learned in the special education workshops—put the child closer to the front of the class or near a window—just aren't working. So what do you do? What tools do you have?

Suppose you discovered that every tool you need to connect with a kid like Jonas is inside of you right now? That it isn't about being properly credentialed, purchasing a new curriculum, investing hours to learn a new teaching style, or even finding a mentor. It's about learning to access your own inner resources, understanding your own sensory system, and discovering how you learn and relate to others. These things will not simply help you reach "unreachable students"; they'll also help you to become the best person that you can possibly be. Best of all, they'll reawaken the true self that initially drew your heart to teaching.

No matter what you are doing to connect with kids with ASD (autism spectrum disorder)—or as we like to say, autism spectrum *difference*—and every child you teach, there is only one constant and that constant is *you*. Every curriculum, every methodology, every approach is funneled through you. The seven keys will show you how to prepare yourself to use all of your training and experience to bring out the best in yourself and in your students.

> I cannot emphasize enough the importance of a good teacher.
>
> *Temple Grandin*

The Seven Keys

As an educator, you are entrusted to make your students more capable to handle new material and to empower them with thinking techniques. You design exercises to increase interaction, engagement, and performance—to unblock the child from his or her real or imagined obstacles. You strive to open up any and all possibilities, just as a locksmith may employ various combinations and keys to open a locked vault.

This is your chosen path as a teacher. Regardless of your teaching experience, you continue to learn, often taking different continuing education programs to keep up with current theories. These courses usually require personal time, energy, and vacation time to study, as well as a financial commitment, and we have heard from teachers who are often already maxed out on all of these areas and are frustrated by the process. Teachers often remark that once they master a new technique, a new, improved version is already being marketed. For teachers who want to keep up and be the best they can be, all this makes for an exhausting and never-ending chase.

The seven keys are groundbreaking in that they bring together powers that you already have as a teacher—sensitivity, commitment, desire to be of service—just as Dorothy had the ruby slippers' power within her all along. You became a teacher to help others, but the first keys we employ are designed to unlock *you* before we unlock autism. These keys, when cultivated, will bring out the highest qualities and effectiveness in your teaching prowess. And all this in less than five minutes a day.

> Put your own oxygen mask on first before putting one on your child.
>
> *Airline advice*

How to Use This Book

As you will see, these seven keys are simple, accessible, and easily applicable to every child with a diagnosis of autism. No matter where you are in your journey as an educator or with your understanding of autism, the seven keys will offer a fresh perspective and much-needed encouragement. You may be overwhelmed by the number of children you have this year and feeling that you just can't deal with a special circumstance when resources are already so stretched and depleted; you may be new to the world of autism and are seeking some navigational aids; or you may be well-versed in all the latest theories and protocols about autism but still feel in need of additional guidance. Or perhaps you're a parent with years of experience or one just starting out. We can assure you that the fundamental principles that comprise the *Seven Keys to Unlock Autism* are beneficial to teachers in all and any circumstances.

This book is organized into three parts. For those of you new to special education, it is recommended that you read from beginning to end, then go back and rehearse the seven keys with each of the exercises. This is not a book that will give you in-depth discourse on autism, the causes, therapies, research, and so on, all of which you can read about in so many informative books and websites. What you will find here is a new approach: its focus is on how a teacher can access resources that will change your own experience of children with autism and enrich the child's experience of you, the teacher.

The invitation is for you to begin this journey to learn about autism as a different way of being. The hope and belief is that in these pages you will find the courage and fortitude to begin to see the world through the eyes of a child with autism.

> Children with autism develop and bloom if their spirits, talents, and self-esteem are not destroyed by bullies, prejudice, "doggie-training," and being forced to be "normal."
>
> *Trisha Van Berkel, South African autism advocate*

The Keys

Each key is described in its own chapter and is a powerful tool on its own. These keys are designed to work individually, in combination, and in progression. Together, the whole is much greater than the sum of its parts.

As we've said before, the seven keys start with you. They guide you on a personal journey first, which in turn unlocks your students. This is the point when anything and everything is possible.

Key One: Set an Intention

Create an internal compass to guide you through the day. This key asks the question, "How am I going to show up and be able to stay calm, centered, and self-regulated regardless of external influences?"

Key Two: Develop Acceptance and Appreciation

To fully accept others, you must first completely accept yourself. Unconditional love and acceptance of individual differences starts with loving and accepting yourself. This key asks the question, "Can I fully accept all of my differences without judgment and be open to see my gifts so that I may honor the gifts in others?"

Key Three: Understand Sensory Profile

This key introduces the experience of autism firsthand through your own senses. This key asks the question, "If I can truly experience the visceral reaction to sensorial overload, will I be better able to relate to the child with autism?"

Key Four: Follow the Leader

Be genuinely interested in what the child is interested in. Let her steer you instead of the other way around and, by so doing, connect with her in a true and deep way. This key asks the question, "Am I willing to be curious and to follow a child without trying to control her?"

Key Five: Include the Child

Value the child's contribution to the classroom dynamic and foster two-way communication. This key asks the question, "Am I totally open to include each and every child, even if it's not according to my plan?"

Key Six: Practice and Preparation Make Progress

Break large tasks into small pieces and rehearse for real-life situations. This key asks the question: "If I give up my perception of perfection and applaud each incremental improvement, can I let go of expectations and timelines that are not appropriate for the child?"

Key Seven: Live Miracle Minded

Approach the child with wonder and joy. This key asks the question, "Regardless of the external situation, can I find the true miracle within each and every child?"

Each key chapter is broken down into the following sections:

- The key within you: A full description and theory that shapes each key

- The lock: A descriptive scenario involving resistance or obstacles you may encounter when not using the key

- An exercise to practice the key

- The unlock: A revisiting of the scenario showing how the key can open the space for moving through obstacles encountered

- From the trenches: A special educator's point of view to give practical applications for the classroom

- Quick keys: Easy-to-review bullets of each key

Before jumping into the seven keys, there is a short primer on autism that offers a brief history and a summary of commonly used abbreviations. The resource guide in Appendixes A and B offer more in-depth material for those seeking further guidance.

Elaine's Story

> There are only two ways to live your life. One is as though nothing is a miracle; the other is as though everything is a miracle.
>
> *Albert Einstein*

I started out as an arts educator and founded Kids On Stage, a children's theater workshop that uses creativity and the arts to bring out the best in all students. In this workshop, we developed self-esteem, self-confidence, and social consciousness as we drew on the kids' strengths and talents and created and produced original musicals based on their ideas and desires. These musicals all had a special twist. For example, instead of doing the traditional show of *Annie*, we made our own version about a homeless girl in East Los Angeles and her gang of homeless friends. We even changed the music to reggae. Soon our classes were packed and attracting children of celebrities such as Dustin Hoffman, Ted Danson, and many others.

I also began teaching drama and movement in some of the top-ranked private schools in Los Angeles, incorporating creativity as part of the regular curriculum. For example, if the students were studying ancient Greece in sixth grade, we would create our own Greek tragedies using contemporary scenarios to enact themes of hubris or divine intervention. Or, if the fourth-grade curriculum was exploring the California Gold Rush, the students would create diaries as if they were actually eight years old and experiencing the westward travels themselves. We developed plays and performed them for the school community.

Soon, I began coaching children on the sets of feature films and television shows. I worked for Disney Studios, CBS Studios, and Nickelodeon and had the privilege of working with some of the most talented kids in Hollywood.

What I learned through my teaching and coaching was to perceive the world through the eyes of the child. This required discipline. I had to perceive the way all children viewed themselves and then do all that I could to bring out their personal best. This core philosophy lent me a unique and profound perspective on autism. But I am getting ahead of myself.

I had been a coach for several years when I discovered that I was not able to give birth biologically. I adopted my son, Neal, from an orphanage in Russia. Neal was twenty-three months old at the time and besides suffering from malnutrition, scurvy, parasites, and liver toxicity, he exhibited all kinds of bizarre behaviors. He spun around in circles, stared at his hand for hours at a time; he opened and closed cabinet doors repeatedly. He spoke no words and did not make eye contact. Today, these behaviors are instantly associated with autism but I didn't know about autism then. (At that time, 1 in 10,000 children were diagnosed with autism. Today it is 1 in 110.) I figured that with good food, vitamins, and lots of love, he would catch up. Over the course of a year, he gained his physical health but he did not catch up in other ways.

Just before his third birthday, Neal was diagnosed with autism and I was thrust from Hollywood into the world of special needs. All of this is chronicled in my first book, *Now I See the Moon: A Mother, a Son, a Miracle* (HarperCollins, 2010).

When Neal was initially diagnosed, he was sentenced to a series of tests, observations, proddings, and questionings. I was told that he had severe autism, mental retardation, with the prognosis of institutionalized living. I was even encouraged to "send him back to Russia," by well-meaning therapists and family members.

We were ultimately guided to a special preschool for children with autism where he might learn rudimentary skills so that he could possibly function—if only at a very low level—in the real world. When we walked in, we saw kids screaming, throwing tantrums, biting, and kicking. Some wore helmets. There was no eye contact. No connection to the other children or the adults.

My gut reaction was to bolt, but I had no other options at the time so, reluctantly, I let Neal stay. Neal was rewarded with M&Ms when he sat still and applauded when he pushed a yellow string through a large blue bead. After weeks in this environment, he still spun in circles, stared at his hand, and made no eye contact. The only difference was that, in the morning, before going to school, he was visibly more anxious.

But then, the faculty of the preschool learned about a doctor on the East Coast named Stanley Greenspan who had developed a new and very different way to work with children on the autistic spectrum. Instead of forcing children to master rote behavioral tasks, he spoke about following a child's lead and understanding the child's sensory system. Though children with autism were thought to be unable to forge human connections, Dr. Greenspan believed that the most important element in helping them was to create meaningful relationships with them.

I brought Neal to Dr. Greenspan. Amazingly, within minutes of being coached by Dr. Greenspan in his office, Neal connected with me more than he had ever done before.

With the doctor's guidance, I would soon come to see that relationships do, in fact, make it possible for children with autism to develop everything they need: they can learn to engage with others, to communicate with gestures, to use ideas creatively, and to think and reflect. Dr. Greenspan also explained that each child with autism has a unique, individualized profile and that it is imperative to see each child for who he or she is and not compare one child to another.

I took to this new method instantly. Dr. Greenspan's method shifted the focus from narrow, behavioral goals to broad foundations, which he calls *milestones* for healthy development. His revolutionary methods are the foundation for the seven keys. Throughout this book, we will explore his developmental approach to learning and also cite the findings of other leading autism educators, therapists, scientists, and medical professionals.

Relating in a New Way with Autism

My challenge over fourteen years ago when I began my efforts to help my son was that very few professionals were working with children in the developmental, individualized way recommended by Dr. Greenspan. When the faculty of the preschool Neal was attending came to accept Dr. Greenspan's developmental, relationship-based approach, they still were not yet able and ready to change their entire curriculum. In fact, any change to an existing educational system is a monumental feat, and even the simplest of adjustments can be like turning an ocean liner around in a narrow harbor. Even with the best intentions, its action is thwarted by the rigid shores. However, I was determined to have this approach implemented immediately for my son, so I pushed with all my might to get the system to change. When it didn't happen, I was left on my own. (Today, this same preschool has developed one of the most respected developmental, relationship-based programs in the country. Time heals everything!)

To School or Not to School, That Is the Question

Steven Hawking says, "When one's expectations are reduced to zero, one really appreciates everything one does have." Without any school options, it was up to me to learn how to educate Neal myself. At the time, most therapists working in autism were trained in the behavioral approach, which is termed *ABA* (applied behavioral analysis). It was the standard. Although this approach works really well for some children, it didn't work for my son and clearly doesn't work for all children with autism. In fact, there is no one-size-fits-all solution for kids with autism. I had no choice but to homeschool Neal and create an appropriate learning environment specifically for him.

When I couldn't convince traditional educators and therapists to help me, I reached out to creative people—actors, musicians, special educators, and others with open minds—in the belief that they would be flexible and open to a progressive, play-based approach. I trained them in everything that I was learning: sensory processing from occupational therapists, speech and language from speech therapists, and how to join a child's world from Dr. Greenspan. I cleared out all the furniture in one room and made it Neal's play- and classroom. We practiced following Neal's lead, and experiencing where he was in the moment. For ten hours a day, seven days a week, we joined Neal in his autistic world. We regarded his behaviors—like spinning in a circle and banging on kitchen cabinets—as his way of communicating. And then we built on those communications.

If he needed to spin in circles, we would take his hands and play "Ring Around the Rosie." Or we would swing him around and around in a net swing. If he needed to throw things, we had a supply of plushy throwing toys that he, at first, threw randomly. We then designed a game with targets made of boxes that he learned to hit. We followed his interests; we allowed his imperatives to direct us. It might have seemed random to a casual observer, but we understood that, in this way, we would progress to effective learning.

This was Dr. Greenspan's magical theory in motion. The approach is to meet the children where they are instead of force them to conform to "our" world. We literally got down on Neal's level to establish a relationship and to support and enhance his true creative nature.

We're not saying that every child with autism needs such drastic measures. But for each child, there are certain milestones that need to be in place before learning can begin. In Neal's case, before he could ever sit in a classroom, he needed to learn to regulate himself. For this to occur, we needed to create a trusting relationship with him, help him learn to regulate his sensory system, and comprehend what he was trying to communicate. Soon, Neal began to relate to us. And soon after that, more traditional learning began. At that point, rather than only follow his interests, we began adult-directed activities. At first we did this for only minutes within each hour; eventually we built up to learning fundamentals throughout his day. To teach him his ABCs we taped large butcher-block paper to the wall and he traced the letters with a paintbrush. Each week, we explored a different letter and learned about the letter in a multisensory, multimodality way. For instance, if the letter of the week was A, we made applesauce, read about airplanes, and explored the feeling of anger. When the letter was B, we played all kinds of ballgames, gave dolls a bath, baked bread, and so on. Using the philosophy of Dr. Greenspan's Floortime model, we created a custom program for our son, one that built on his strengths and supported his areas of need. Autism is a highly individualized condition and requires as highly an individualized approach to bring out the best in the child.

Neal began making eye contact and expressing his feelings. He was able to regulate his body long enough to complete a lesson. His nonverbal communication skills opened the door for him to socialize. He was prepared to enter the school system. Starting with baby steps, Neal first attended a special ed class, starting with just an hour a day and building to nearly a half day. In time, with the help of a one-on-one aide, Neal was able to spend part of his day in a general education third-grade classroom. He used a choice board to express his needs and answer questions in class. By fifth grade, Neal and his one-on-one aide were spending their entire day in a regular education environment led by a wonderful teacher, Mr. Sanchegrain, or Mr. S as he was affectionately called. In *Seven Keys to Unlock Autism*, we will provide insights into how Mr. S worked out this unique educational experience. You will meet him and other teachers like him who refused to view Neal's autism as a burden or as a condition that would detract from their class-rooms. Instead, these gifted teachers understood that Neal's presence in their class was value added for their typically developing students.

Putting Myself at the Top of the List

As Neal was progressing, I was falling apart. I had put so much time and energy into helping him become the best he could be that I found that I had become a shell of my own existence. My marriage was in shambles, my friendships lacking, and my financial situation close to desperate. I had forgotten the rule of self-care. I mention this because so many well-intentioned and effective edu-cators burn out because they are so involved with the care of others that they forget to care for themselves. For my survival—and Neal's—I needed to put the focus on myself. I needed to explore my own needs, set my own intentions, and stop beating myself up for not being "perfect." That's why the second, essential key is to develop acceptance. Through my own therapeutic process I learned to focus on myself and my own needs and to truly love and accept myself. You know the old adage, "you can't truly love another person until you love yourself first." Well, this was proved to me. One of my mentors likened the process to the story of the goose who laid the golden egg, pointing out that there could be no egg if the goose was cooked!

And so I focused on my life and was quick to observe how my marriage was no longer serving me or the family. Instead of feeling supported and in partnership, it was an additional drain to what precious energy I could muster up. When I realized this relationship was an impediment to my ability to function as a mother, and a person for that matter, I ended my marriage and needed to go back to work.

The Miracle Project Is Born

I didn't want to go back to full-time coaching on film and television, so I searched within myself for what I should do. It quickly became very clear to me: teach acting, singing, and dance to children with special needs. At first I scoffed at my inner director, thinking, "I have no degrees in special education, no professional training." But then a friend encouraged me to apply for a grant to create a theater program for children with special needs. This appealed to me. I not only needed the money, but now, as a single mom with a child with autism, I was isolated and alone and in need of community.

I told the grant committee that my proposal was not only to create a theater program for children but also to also create an inclusive community. I wanted to provide a place for all family members: there would be parent discussion groups, and parents would be encouraged to help with costumes, sets, programs, and publicity. The idea was to create a safe, dynamic, and nurturing environment for families of children with special needs.

I set out a goal to create an original musical to showcase the unique and wonderful nature of children who have special needs. When they create it and perform it, their beauty will come shining through. It will reaffirm two things I deeply believe: that the creative process can transform lives, and that "different" doesn't mean "less" and can often mean "more."

I wrote the grant in just a few days, and with beginner's luck, it was awarded to me. I began to create The Miracle Project, a theater and film program for children with autism and other special needs and their typically developing siblings and peers.

I committed to training more than twenty people to work with twenty kids who have autism and other special needs. I also committed to writing and directing an original musical for the kids to star in. "How can I do this?" I wondered, as my sense of panic rose. I needed staff and volunteers, so I gathered together a group of actors, singers, and dancers who had little to no experience working with children with special needs. With the help of Dr. Sarita Santos, a professor of special education, I led a twenty-hour training program for twenty-five staff members and volunteers, coaching them in what is now known as the seven keys to unlock autism. I shared with them everything I had learned about myself, about Neal, about creativity, and told them about Dr. Greenspan's theories. I wanted them to see autism as something extraordinary. I wanted them to bring open hearts and open minds to the world of children with autism. I wanted them to be loving and nonjudgmental and willing to be the student as well as the teacher.

I still use this training method. I start out with the most basic principle: I ask my volunteers, staff, and others to regard autism not as a disorder but simply as a different way of being. At each training session we begin with the centering exercise and meditation that I do at home: we breathe together and let go of all the thoughts and events that occurred prior to gathering.

I have found that doing this makes a world of difference when I am with Neal. I tell them how Neal senses if my mind or heart is agitated or if I'm not really paying attention. I want the volunteers and staff to know that it's of critical importance when they work with the kids to be totally calm and totally in the here and now. You will learn about this in Key One.

I share aspects of my personal journey. I tell them the importance of learning to accept what you fear, of embracing what you dread. I tell them about the freedom that comes when you shake hands with the things that frighten you most. These are the principles behind Key Two.

I also want our team to understand the sensory system. For this, I create an exercise through which they'll experience sensory overwhelm. You will go through this exercise and others like it in Key Three.

Next, I teach how to follow a child's lead and to playfully challenge kids to expand their abilities, which is the foundation for Key Four.

I still remember vividly the first night of The Miracle Project. The volunteers were excited but also nervous. They wanted to help the children, yet they didn't feel confident that they had what it takes to truly be present with them. I invited them to just show up with lots of energy and to trust themselves. They did. We gathered together before the children arrived; calmed our bodies with a guided meditation; shared our intentions to be open, playful, and calm; and then we tuned into our sensory systems to become aware of the sights, sounds, and smells around us; readying our hearts for the children to enter.

That first evening was chaotic. Fifteen kids took part. Some did not want to leave their parents or enter the room. Others entered reluctantly, holding on to their mother's legs. Some parents didn't want to let go of their kids even if the kids were fine. When a few of the kids hid under tables, I encouraged a volunteer to hide under the table with them. Others ran in circles. We turned this into a game of hide and go seek.

Then, we danced together, moving across the floor with hops, skips, slides, and "silliness." Danny, my friend Michele's son, let one of our volunteers roll his wheelchair. He glided gleefully. I gave each child an opportunity to do his or her own special movement. Kids flapped or walked on tip toes or did other usually "socially unacceptable" behaviors. As they executed these movements, we applauded them. We joined them. We turned their hops and slides into dance that included using their thoughts, movements, and impromptu sounds. This is Key Five.

We broke down all adult-directed activities into small, manageable tasks, which we will discuss in Key Six. Finally, we celebrated each child's abilities to be part of the group whether his or her contribution was large or small, bringing us to Key Seven.

We told each parent all the terrific things their child did that day. To some of these parents, it was the first positive thing they heard about their child in years. At the end of the evening, parents gathered their child's belongings and left, smiling as they departed. Then, as a team, the staff and volunteers discussed what worked and what didn't work and shared their feelings about the evening. Everyone was energized and exuberant even though we'd just led a rigorous ninety-minute class, not stopping for even a moment. Their fears were replaced with a glowing sense of peace and accomplishment. They had unlocked the world of autism.

In less than eleven weeks, these very same children, many of whom had never participated in any group activity before, would come together and create a play. Ten weeks later, they filmed a movie, created seven original songs, and helped write an original script that they performed *live* in a packed, state-of-the-art theater in Los Angeles. It was extraordinary: every child performed, every parent glowed with joy, and the audience gave standing ovations, overcome with tears to see these inspiring children defy all expectations of what children with autism can do.

During the course of the final rehearsals, a group of filmmakers endorsed by Cure Autism Now, now a part of Autism Speaks, asked to visit our class. Apparently, the word was out that we were doing things that "experts" had deemed undoable for children with autism: participating in a loud group, effortlessly making transitions from one activity to another, being spontaneous and emotional, showing empathy, accepting adult-directed activity, and more. We had no idea that what we were doing was considered "impossible." We were just using the seven keys and showing up each session with open hearts and open minds.

The next year, The Miracle Project and its methods were chronicled in the double Emmy Award–winning HBO documentary, *Autism: The Musical*. Since *Autism: The Musical* aired on HBO in April 2008, I have received thousands of e-mails requesting The Miracle Project in communities around the world and from educators, like you, who want to better understand autism. Soon after its initial screening, I asked Diane Isaacs, a film producer and mother of a student in The Miracle Project, to partner with me and help make these methods available to others. *Autism: The Musical* is now used in universities, summer camps, hospitals, and so on as a training film to inspire parents and teachers alike and demonstrate what is possible for children with autism.

I have been privileged to speak throughout the United States and Canada and even at the United Nations about what I learned from my work with my son and other children with autism. The seven keys are being taught internationally with Diane Isaacs, and our music director Karen Howard recently returned from leading workshops for parents and professionals in India. The very same children who at one time were too frightened to walk into a room with other children are now performing in front of hundreds of people, and performed and were even honored at the United Nations. They were recently honored at Carnegie Hall! I have witnessed firsthand how anyone who is willing can be taught these seven keys. I even trained Hollywood talent agents and business executives who had no experience with children who have autism, giving them, in a two-hour workshop, an abridged version of the seven keys. They then spent the afternoon with kids on the autism spectrum creating stories, songs, and dances that they performed with them later that afternoon. All within less than six hours! If these business folk can connect with children with autism, imagine what you, as an educator can do.

You may be thinking, "Okay, I can see how this approach may work in a creative arts atmosphere, but how can these methods be implemented in a classroom?" Fortunately, in my travels and those of my coauthor, Diane Issacs, we have been privileged to meet some of the most influential people illuminating autism today, among them DanaKae Bonahoom, Temple Grandin, Stanley Greenspan, Carol Gray, Darlene Hanson, Portia Iverson, Barry Prizant, Ricki Robinson, Stephen Shore, Serena Weider, and many others. We have witnessed the benefits of developmental learning as practiced in some of the most respected schools in the country. In this book, we will give you a bird's-eye view of some very exciting programs and educators. We found that whenever we discovered teachers who were having great impact on their students, they were instinctively using the seven keys! All we have done is systematized what is already working so that you, too, can make meaningful connections with children who have autism.

On the DVD

Please take a few minutes to watch the DVD included in the back of this book. The videos included will show you some of the seven keys in action.

Seven Keys to Unlock Autism

Part One

Autism 101

Primer
Autism Through a Different Lens

*Autism is not a puzzle, nor a disease. Autism is a
challenge, but certainly not a devastating one.*
                                        Trisha Van Berkel

There are still so many questions about the cause of autism—
whether it is environmental, genetic, systemic, biochemical,
or all of the above. With all the advanced medical research of
autism, there is still not a found cause or cure for autism but rather
recommendations of therapies, interventions, dietary adjustments,
supplements, pharmaceuticals, or an individualized combination.

The prevailing symbol for autism is a puzzle piece, which indicates that there are many parts to the whole picture, and most
often, not all the pieces are on the table. Although great strides
have been made in diagnostic education, there remains a gray zone
as to exactly what defines autism because the spectrum's criteria
are not etched in stone, nor are any two children with autism the
same. So from cause to effect to cure, it remains a puzzle for experts,
parents, and child alike.

We prefer to use the symbol of the butterfly, which starts out
as a caterpillar, retreats into a chrysalis, and then emerges in its
own time into something extraordinary. Yes, autism can be seen
not as puzzle, problem, or disorder but as a wondrous and different
way of being. It's all in the perception.

In its most simple terms, autism is a neurological difference or *disorganization* that affects the development and functioning of the brain. Autism is usually distinguished with sensory-processing and motor-planning challenges (which in lay terms refers to the ability to remember a series of steps and execute them) as well as expressive and social issues that may affect speech and language, coordination, and learning.

With today's diagnostic awareness, it is usually diagnosed around the age of eighteen months to two years, although symptoms can often be recognized in hindsight from birth. Key developmental milestones are missed by the child, and certain developmental skills such as language or eye contact are lost. Autism affects the child's social and communication development most acutely. The cognitive profile of a child with autism is as unique as neurotypical children. In some cases, cognitive levels are affected and in others mental acumen may be heightened.

Sensory processing is how we organize our sensory input from our environment. Regulation of the senses can also be unpredictable and inconsistent for children with autism. For people with autism, the sounds, touch, smells, sights, and everything they hear may be perceived as distorted—often turned up very high or down very low. A conversation in the room next door can be amplified to a high volume while a person talking directly in front of the child can be zoned out. A simple lamp can appear like a powerful strobe to a child with visual hypersensitivity. The individual variations create a unique puzzle with hyper- or hyposensitivities to the environment, and it may change from one moment to another. Such irregulation of sensory input can redirect cognitive functions and communication abilities.

Stephen Shore, an adult autistic and professor at Adelphi University, refers to autism as a "different way of being." Looked at this way, autism is neither good nor bad—it's simply different, and it is the so-called typically developing (commonly referred to within the autism community as *neurotypicals*) who need to accept and learn about these differences.

The component of speech and language includes oral and non-verbal communication. When we communicate with one another we use receptive and expressive language. Receptive language refers to a person receiving language. It involves a level of cognition, which is what the person actually understands. Expressive language is the ability to communicate wants, needs, and responses—the ability to be understood. These areas work together to create a complete communication. The most obvious way to express language is through speech. However, children with autism often have challenges with speech, so other ways to communicate can be done through sign language, pointing to words and pictures on a communication board, or formulating written messages on a computer screen. People with autism may not be able to express themselves in a typical way, but they may have a high level of cognition or understanding. There are many individuals who have been thought to be mentally retarded due to their lack of communication skills, yet once they obtain a way to express themselves, their intellect is astonishingly developed and sometimes superior to their peers. Most "behaviors" are, in actuality, efforts to communicate. Barry Prizant, an internationally renowned speech and language pathologist, goes as far as to claim that "all behavior is communication."

Motor processing and regulation is the ability to understand and process body movements. When a person is eating and puts food on a fork, the brain sends a signal that moves the hand toward the mouth. With people with autism, that movement may be delayed or their body may need additional support via prompts, reminders, or cues to execute the seemingly simple movement. Motor processing requires mental planning, which may be erratic or impaired with an individual with autism. It has been predicted that many children with autism have different wiring of the brain and body, with some synapses developed within the normal range and others overdeveloped or underdeveloped. This affects the think-plan-act pattern that occurs naturally for individuals who do not have autism.

The Different Viewpoints of Elaine and Diane

Although the autistic spectrum, with its myriad levels and categories, has been defined as a disability, we seek to find the abilities within each child. We have worked with so many unique children with autism and have found a gem inside each and every one. We are not here to minimize the challenges that are inherent with the condition. We acknowledge the difficulties that arise on a daily level. We do not bypass the many daunting questions that parents and teachers have about the child that do not appear to have immediate answers. What we choose to focus on is that every challenge has a silver lining, the double edge that can be as sweet as it is bitter. We honor the gifts of autism—not the outstanding talents that a small percentage display in art, music, or in-depth special interests—but the gifts of being honest, being in the moment, being highly sensitive. Mostly we have gratitude for the gifts we receive when we open our hearts to those who experience the world differently.

There is a myth that children with autism do not show empathy. We have found that quite to the contrary. Children with autism are among the most sensitive beings we have ever encountered. They may show their sensitivities in less-than-typical ways—but they don't strive to be "normal." Their bumper sticker should be "typical is overrated."

A Brief History

Since about 2000, autism has become a highly visible thread in the fabric of our society. As with most things in life, this did not happen overnight. From its earliest days, autism has baffled the medical and scientific communities as they struggled to answer what it actually is as well as the complicated matters of how to define its diagnostic features, what causes it, and how to cure it. Today, we are fortunate to have an ongoing discussion of autism in scientific and medical circles and well-funded research. Folks who actually have autism are now teaching us about autism—but it wasn't always this way. Here is a brief account of the highly dramatic and sometimes horror-filled evolution of the understanding of autism.

The word *autism* came into being in 1911 when it was first used by the Swiss psychiatrist Eugen Bleuler. *Autism* is based on the Greek word *autos*, meaning *self* and was applied to patients who seemed removed from social interaction. Bleuler loosely translated autism as an "escape from reality" and, in his understanding, autism overlapped with schizophrenia and mental retardation.

In the 1940s, Leo Kanner of Johns Hopkins University borrowed Bleuler's label and diagnosed patients with *autism* based on emotional, antisocial, and isolating behaviors. At the same time, the Austrian scientist Hans Asperger coined the term *Asperger's* to differentiate those children with autism who were highly verbal. Although these two diagnoses appeared in medical journals at this time, it would take decades before the medical profession would truly understand the diverse developmental symptoms and apply proper diagnostic techniques. In the meantime, the learning curve as to the what, why, and how to identify, address, and treat took many wrong turns. One such misguided discourse occurred under the leadership of Bruno Bettelheim, director of University of Chicago's Orthogenic School, a home for disturbed children. In one study, he compared children with autism to feral children, as if children with autism shared animalistic behaviors like wolf babies in India. He attributed the incidence of such untamable behaviors to early emotional deprivation from the parents. Rather than seeing autism as the neurological condition it is, in his didactic publication, *The Empty Fortress: Infantile Autism and the Birth of the Self* (1967), he likened the parent of an autistic child to a "devouring witch, an infanticidal king, and an SS guard in a concentration camp," and continued his parental blame game stating that "the precipitating factor in infantile autism is the parent's wish that his child should not exist."

Bettelheim blindly led the understanding of autism into darkness and horror. He was a follower of Freud, the father of modern psychology, who believed that all psychological issues stemmed from childhood trauma. Building on the misguided systemic beliefs of Bettelheim, Dr. Kanner witnessed a consistent coldness on the part of the mothers, and although he believed autism to be somewhat innate in the child, he perpetuated the myth of icy parenting as the source of autism for years to follow, coining the label *refrigerator mother*.

Fortunately, parent advocacy groups with scientific support have since debunked such a ridiculous premise. Still, the stigma it created was not easily dissipated and parental guilt for not doing enough for their atypically developing child remains commonplace today. Even now, and all too often, blame for autism is directed at the child's parents. This has taken on a different form in that parents now do so many interventions with their children in an attempt to fix them and then blame themselves when their children are not "cured."

The 1960s and 1970s were rife with more missteps and misunderstandings. The medical community concentrated their research on medications to cure autism. Experimental and oftentimes radical drugs were administered, including the psychedelic LSD. Neurological treatments such as electric shock therapy were used. Children were literally tied down to control their impulsive behaviors and locked in closets. In 1974, *Psychology Today* cited one doctor for his method of dealing with the problems of children with autism: "We spank them hard."

Throughout these decades, the primary objective of psychologists, therapists, and teachers was to behaviorally control children with autism through rigid and severe reward-and-consequence tactics. It had not yet occurred to most members of the medical profession that autism was something more than what they mistook it for: a form of mental retardation and social dysfunction.

In the 1970s, the true pioneers of autism reform emerged with new therapeutic models to address autism. Their work is offered through therapists and schools today:

- Ivar Lovaas, a clinical psychologist at UCLA, began to dig deeper into the mystery of autism and came up with what is called ABA (applied behavioral analysis). He was one of the first to provide evidence that the behavior of autistic children could be modified through breaking down goals into small manageable tasks.

- Stanley Greenspan, a renowned theoretician, diagnostician, and clinician of child development, built the DIR (developmental, individual-difference, relationship-based) approach, which focuses on emotional and relationship development techniques. His method calls for following the child's lead to establish a trusting relationship between the child and parent, teacher, or therapist.

- Eric Schopler, a professor of psychiatry and psychology at the University of North Carolina and a pioneer in humane and effective treatment of autism protocols, designed an educational school model with a structured and visual environment he called TEACH (treatment and education of autistic and related communication-handicapped children).

- Barry Prizant and his colleagues developed the SCERTS (social communication, emotional regulation, and transactional support) model, which is an innovative educational model for working with children with ASD and their families by building competence in these areas.

- RDI (relationship development intervention) is a therapeutic training by Steven Gutstein, a psychologist with experience in traditional behavioral approaches for treatment, who saw that many of his children lacked the ability to connect on an emotional level. He created a family-based therapeutic approach to train parents to guide the cognitive, social, and emotional development of their own child. Through the framework of a unique, dynamic intelligent curriculum, children become motivated to seek out new challenges and overcome their fear of change.

All of these protocols are still highly regarded and used today. Their common denominator is to get a jumpstart with early intervention and to recognize the individual nature of each child.

Often parents will be committed to one protocol or another. Some of these programs require 100 percent allegiance to following their procedures. However, the National Research Council (2001) has recognized that there is no evidence that any one categorical approach is more effective than other approaches and also that approaches are likely to overlap. The committee recommended that children with ASD engage in programs that provide social instruction across a variety of settings.

Usually, a combination of many therapies is required. It may include sensory integration, physical therapy, fine and gross motor development, speech and language, play therapy, occupational therapy, signed speech, cognitive therapy, behavioral therapy, as well as other approaches such as a casein-gluten free diet, natural supplements, pharmacology, and acupuncture.

Inspirational Stories

The history of autism contains many inspiring stories. In the early 1950s, Temple Grandin was diagnosed with autism and brain damage as a child. Her mother, Eustacia Cutler, found teachers to work with her starting in nursery school. Temple was blessed to have supportive mentors who looked beyond her disabilities and recognized her potential. Not only did she learn to speak, but she also developed into an accomplished student. Ultimately, she transcended all expectations with her visionary designs for humane cattle farming, which revolutionized the livestock business. She is a best-selling author of many books featuring her astute insight, such as *Animals in Translation* and *Animals Make Us Human*. Her story is an outstanding model of the way in which a person with autism can be encouraged to employ particular gifts for the betterment of all.

Stephen Shore, now an international speaker and professor at Adelphi University, was born in 1947, at a time when autism was not even in the dictionary, much less in the medical curriculum. He was diagnosed as "that quirky kid who made strange sounds" rather than one on the autistic spectrum. Stephen was nonverbal until the age of four and deemed "too sick" to attend school. It was recommended that he be placed in an institution for life. Yet, with the support of his parents and key teachers who saw his potential, Stephen bravely navigated his way through the public school system. In the process, he gleaned how to teach children on the autism spectrum and, equally important, what to avoid when teaching them. He completed his doctorate and is now a professor of autism at Adelphi University as well as a motivational speaker and internationally published author of the compelling autobiography, *Beyond the Wall: Personal Experiences with Autism and Asperger Syndrome*, and the expert contributor to the series, *Understanding Autism for Dummies*.

The success stories of Temple and Stephen testify to the fact that many remarkable children will emerge from classrooms led by teachers who refuse to see autism as a limitation. Such teachers inspire children to follow and realize their passions and dreams.

Another remarkable person with autism is Wyatt Isaacs, Diane's son, who has become a global ambassador for autism at the age of fifteen and is one of the children with autism featured in *Autism: The Musical*. With his blonde hair, blue eyes, and freckles, Wyatt looks at first like the "boy next door." He's sweet, shy, and a little self-conscious. But within minutes of conversation with him, you realize that he has an old-soul wisdom, a knowingness and sensitivity far beyond his years. "Your head tells you what you want," he says, "but your heart tells you what you need." Wyatt spoke to hundreds of international ambassadors at the United Nations, recorded with Stephen Stills and Jack Black, sang at Carnegie Hall, and has taught theater to children with autism in Ethiopia and India. His mission is to share the gifts of autism on a global level.

> Research demonstrates that autistic traits are distributed into the nonautistic population; some people have more of them, some have fewer. History suggests that many individuals whom we would today diagnose as autistic—some severely so—contributed profoundly to our art, our math, our science, and our literature.
>
> *Morton Gernsbacher, parent of an autistic child*

Wyatt is perceptive and philosophical about autism. He was twelve years old when he said, "Often people—mostly adults, but kids, too—completely miss seeing the kids with autism. They judge them by how they are on the outside—kids with autism sometimes flap and spin, some cannot speak or they talk too loud—they look 'weird.' That is what most people see—where I see the beautiful flower inside. Trust me. It's in there if you take the time to really look."

Later, we will tell you more about Wyatt and introduce you to several other verbal and nonverbal autistics who at first glance appear totally in their own worlds and even exhibit unpredictable behaviors, but are capable of profound thought and wisdom through typing and augmentative communication systems. This book is a tour of the lovely, secret garden within so many young minds and hearts.

> Education is an ornament in prosperity and a refuge in adversity.
>
> *Aristotle, 4th century BC*

Autism's Alphabet Soup

As you go along with the seven keys, we'll make reference to certain diagnoses, therapies, and administrative nomenclature. Here is a short list of some that may come across your desk.

The Diagnoses

ASD (autism spectrum disorder) is a group of neurodevelopmental disabilities with unique challenges in social interaction and communication. It includes autism, Rhett's syndrome, and Asperger's syndrome. ASD is an umbrella label for the many facets and manifestations of autism and autismlike behaviors.

Asperger's syndrome is also part of the autistic spectrum. It affects a child's ability to socialize and communicate effectively with others; however, children with Asperger's usually develop strong interests in specific subjects with high levels of understanding. People diagnosed with Asperger's often display limited, repetitive communication, redirecting conversation to be within their comfort range of the subject they have developed. They may not understand jokes or metaphors, as they tend to take things very literally. In a classroom these students may at times appear lost or ask questions that seem off target; however, their cognitive function and astute awareness may be fully engaged. Asperger's covers a wide range of abilities and is often hard to observe from the child's functional appearance.

PDD-NOS (pervasive developmental disorder, not otherwise specified) is a condition on the autism spectrum in which children will exhibit some, but not all, of the symptoms associated with classic autism. Some of the symptoms can include difficulty socializing with others, repetitive behaviors, and heightened sensitivities to certain stimuli. PDD-NOS is a more general diagnosis for autism. It basically states that there are developmental problems and no one specific area can be identified as the dominating factor. This diagnosis is very difficult for parents to receive for their child as it leaves many unanswered questions.

Nonverbal, apraxia, or fluency impaired is characterized in children with autism who lack the ability to speak. It is not a diagnosis that assumes the child cannot express himself. There are various technologies and systems to accommodate expressive communication through typing, letter boards, picture boards, voice-activated typing machines, iPads with specifically designed applications, and sign language. Just because the child cannot speak doesn't mean she cannot listen, understand, and voice her thoughts. Often, the silent one has the most to say.

MR (mental retardation) is not part and parcel with autism. Many children with autism have highly developed cognitive ability; others are on a level with their typically developing peers.

Autism is not defined by any particular level of intelligence or cognitive capacity. It is a unique rewiring of how the brain processes sensory input and relates that to expressive behavior. Some children carry the autism label with MR, but it is as individual as it is with people who are not autistic.

Specific Therapies

Physical therapists are health-care professionals who diagnose and treat students who have medical problems or other health-related conditions, illnesses, or injuries that limit their abilities to move and perform functional activities in the school setting. These therapists assist students in using their bodies in successful and rewarding ways through physical therapy (PT). If students have difficulty using their arms or legs, a physical therapist will develop a plan for mobility in the classroom and at the school site. Students may be pulled out of class for this service.

Occupational therapy (OT) helps students improve their basic motor functions and reasoning abilities. An occupational therapist supports the student's movement in the educational setting. Simple tasks such as holding a pencil or using scissors may require the student to move in ways that are challenging. Occupational therapy may be done in tandem with another student to foster game playing and social motivation. Students may be pulled out of class for this service.

Sensory integration (SI) is a refined form of OT to help the student process sensory input. Often, students with autism have sensory integration disorder, which is a neurological disorder resulting from the brain's inability to integrate information received from the body's five basic sensory systems that detect sights, sounds, smell, tastes, temperatures, pain, and the position and movements of the body. The two lesser-known systems are the vestibular and proprioceptive. The vestibular system deals with balance and the way that the body moves. Proprioception is the awareness of where the body is in space and in relation to surrounding objects.

The nervous system needs to integrate these two systems through the senses and mind-body functions. Senses that are very sensitive or underresponsive can cause anxiety and difficulty to a student with SI disorder. For example, if students with SI disorder are very sensitive to sound, they may experience the sound of another student's sneeze as so painful and piercing that it causes them to scream. Why are they screaming? Perhaps the sneeze literally hurts their ears and their entire nervous system. In other words, their scream is not an overreaction or an inappropriate response. It's a direct response to the way they experience that sneeze. Two informative books on this subject are *Sensory Integration and the Child* by Jean Ayres (Western Psychological Services, 1980) and *The Out-of-Sync Child* by Carol Stock Kranowitz (Penguin, 1998).

Speech and language (SL) or speech pathology assesses, diagnoses, treats, and helps to prevent disorders related to speech, language, cognitive communication, voice, swallowing, and fluency. These therapists often work with students who cannot produce speech sounds at all or cannot produce them clearly.

A speech pathologist works one-on-one or in a group setting with students who have difficulty receiving or expressing language. For instance, a student could have weak muscles in his mouth that prevents him from saying certain words or sounds. A speech pathologist would work with the student to strengthen his muscles and sound production. Students are often pulled out of class for this service.

Adapted physical education (APE) are PE activities for students with limited mobility or movement. The activities directed by the APE instructor help students increase their physical capabilities, such as catching, throwing, or kicking a ball with appropriate targets. Students are often pulled out of class to attend APE or it can be done during regular PE times. It is often done as a group activity to foster interaction and peer encouragement.

The Administrative Terms

The individualized education program (IEP) is a legally binding agreement between the parent and the school district that spells out exactly what services a student will need and why. The IEP is created by a team that consists of teachers, therapists, administrators, parents, and, if appropriate, the student.

Each individualized plan may include "pull-out therapies" when a child is taken out of the classroom and given different resources and interventions to help the student in an academic environment. It may also include a one-on-one aide, sensory strategies, modified curriculum, and so on. The IEP sets individual goals in educational areas as well as behavioral and transitional aspects.

Individuals with Disabilities Education Act (IDEA) is a law ensuring services to children with disabilities throughout the United States. IDEA governs how states and public agencies provide early intervention, special education, and related services to eligible infants, toddlers, children, and youth with disabilities.

IDEA provides legal guidelines that protect the rights of children with disabilities in the educational setting. It sets standards and expectations of how educational services should be delivered. It is important to know the IDEA guidelines each year to best service students with disabilities.

The level of service ascribed to a child is based on local legislation and regional service organizations that are fiscally sponsored by the state or privately funded. Funding is often tricky as many needed services may not be considered eligible based on standardized protocols. Check with your local regional centers that have state funding and offer services for eligible children. Some programs have scholarship funds that may be offered to cover tuition based on financial needs.

What's in a Name?

There is a question about nomenclature. Should we say "a child with autism" or "an autistic child" or "he has autism" or "he is autistic"? "People-first" language dictates that we say, "a child with autism." Many parents prefer this. My son, Neal, now almost seventeen years old, has always referred to himself as autistic; sometimes he'll type that "my autism" caused him to do certain things. In this book, we will use all terms: an autistic, a person with autism, and so on. It's worth noting that Stephen Shore, an adult with autism, cites a recent poll in which 75 percent of adults with autism preferred to be called simply "autistic." As each child is a unique individual, simply see what the child and parent prefer.

There are still many parents who prefer that their child does not know that he or she has autism. It is always best practice to respect each parent's requests.

Part Two

The Seven Keys

Set an Intention

I believe that the choice to be excellent begins with
aligning your thoughts and words with the intention
to require more from yourself.

Oprah Winfrey

We live in a culture of trophy worship. Success—and beyond that, winning—are the ultimate prizes, which prompt us to focus on the destination rather than the journey and subscribe to the false notion that the ends justify the means.

Of course, it's commendable to set a plan and to have standards and expectations as long as we don't allow them to lead to despair and feelings of failure when the "prize" is not won. This key unlocks your ability to set an intention and follow through with it no matter what is going on in the classroom.

An intention is not a goal; it is an aim that guides the action. Setting a goal, such as we'll get through three multiplication tables today, locks you in and makes you rigid; setting an intention, such as I want the kids to enjoy learning math, allows you to let go and be guided by what happens *in* the classroom, *with* each child, *in the moment*.

You can see that *intentions* and *goals* are quite different. *Webster's* defines *intention* as "a determination to act in a certain way." *The Oxford English Dictionary* defines *goal* as follows:

21

"point marking end of a race; objective of effort or ambition; destination."

Goals are a necessary feature of life in our schools, especially when it comes to work in special education, as anyone who has attended an IEP meeting knows. The IEP team sets specific and measurable goals for the student with special needs. These goals will be worked on throughout the school year. The goals help guide the academic and the social-emotional program for the child. They are quantifiable milestones along the long and winding road of learning and personal development.

Goals certainly have their place. We set them in the hope that our children will rise to them and perform to the best of their ability. The problem is that goals can also be counterproductive if they do not fit the profile of a child. They can place pressure on a child that ultimately inhibits his ability to learn. Or they can be set so low that a child's abilities are not fully actualized. Because we are ever evolving, so should any goals that are set, and so we should realize that they are malleable guides rather than tangible fixtures.

Consequently, how is setting a goal different from setting an intention? Setting a goal establishes a specific outcome that must be achieved for success to be declared. This goal may lock you into a rigid paradigm of success or failure, which can lead to disappointment. A goal is about *doing*; an intention is about *being*.

> In the universe, there is an immeasurable indescribable force which shamans call intent, and absolutely everything that exists in the entire cosmos is attached to intent by a connecting link.
>
> *Carlos Castaneda*

Elaine recalls a heartbreaking story about William, a nonverbal autistic teen whose featured goal in his IEP since he was six years old was to "tie his shoes." For the next seven years, occupational therapists, behaviorists, and volunteers worked endlessly to help him achieve this coveted goal. They believed that they needed to triumph over the fact that William had severe motor-planning and sequencing challenges that made reaching this goal extremely difficult. William resisted this painful process, but despite his rant behaviors and tantrums, he was repeatedly coerced into attempting this task, rewarded with M&Ms, hugs, and smiles each step of the way. Finally, shortly after his thirteenth birthday, he finally wrapped one lace around the other and shaped it into two sweet lovely bows, causing his parents to shout with joy. Mission accomplished!

It would be two years before William learned to type and could articulate what he felt when he finally tied his shoes. As his parents, therapists, and teachers jumped for joy, William described it as the worst day of his life.

He wrote about how being coerced into shoe tying had been a daily source of humiliation. He asked his parents why they just didn't go out and get him shoes that fastened with Velcro! He wondered why it was so much more important to them that he do this menial task than to truly acknowledge his interests and notice what was important to him. Their drive to this goal somehow made William feel invalidated. His success with laces was not of value to him and reminded him daily that they were not listening to him.

William continued to express that he would have much rather had his team spend those hours reading books to him, discussing the current events, and learning age-appropriate materials. But you see, he did not have the words at the time. He was communicating as best he could with his behaviors. Clearly, William had completely different goals than his parents.

We might always ask the question of a goal, "How important is it?" In William's case, a quick run to the sporting goods store and a pair of Velcro sneakers would have saved years of endless upheaval.

We are human beings, not human doings.

As you know, there are many variables and unpredictable occurrences in your classroom, especially when working with children with autism. This means that it is essential that you remain the reliable constant for the child. Although there are a number of things you can physically control in the classroom environment, such as lighting, spatial design, and sound, to minimize misdirected sensory stimulation, you cannot control the behaviors, actions, and reactions of the individuals in your class.

The only thing you can fully control in your classroom is your own attitude and your own state of being. This starts with your conviction *to behave and react in* a certain way, no matter what is going on around you. If you set your intention to be unruffled and relaxed no matter what happens, you'll be able to deal with a child who is having a particularly rough day.

You know this dance very well: child has a meltdown; teacher tries to force child to sit and calm down; teacher gets upset; child gets worse. Well, what if you tried something different? Child has a meltdown; teacher calmly breathes and encourages child to breathe; student calms down.

What if you decided to leave home your serious side for the day and set your intention to be playful? Your teaching will have a levity to it, and you can cultivate your students' participation in playful learning. Maybe you push the desks aside and build a pretend campfire in the middle of the room and teach in a circle with camp activities between subjects. Maybe you create a tribe and have students role-play the chief, warriors, buffalo hunters, gatherers, and so on.

If there is stress and behavioral upheaval, if you approach it through playfulness, the energy of the class will follow your lead and often a greater problem will be averted. Other intentions may be to be patient, empathetic, and compassionate. Imagine yourself practicing these intentions. Students with autism respond particularly well when the teacher's intention is to be calm.

Paradoxically, once you let go of the goal and let your intention guide you, you will be more likely to achieve more goals in the long run. For example at The Miracle Project, the goal is to create a musical for the kids to write and star in. The intention is for the children to feel comfortable. If Elaine comes in on the first day attempting to read lines, block scenes, and rehearse a play, nothing will happen and there will never be a show. If she comes with the intention to let them feel comfortable, she creates a warm and cozy environment for the children to feel safe to be themselves. She encourages them to hop and skip across the floor; to be in their own space until they are ready to be part of a group; and she takes time to discover what interests them. All the activities are directed to creating a comfort zone for the new kids. Eventually, over the course of the next twenty-plus weeks, a musical production will come out of it that will far exceed the goal she set initially. It may not appear that a full-on musical can come to fruition from the early sessions, but opening night eventually comes and surpasses everyone's expectations of what is possible for a child with autism to do.

It is essential that you remain the reliable constant for the child.

Key One begins with addressing the way you, as a teacher, caregiver, parent, friend, or neighbor, prepare yourself before you even meet up with a child with autism. Remember that this has nothing to do with fixing or controlling the child or manipulating the environment. It is all about you being the steady and persistent compass for navigating the changing waters of a dynamic classroom.

Even if a child is overwhelmed or having a tantrum, if you can be the consistent "calm within the storm," you will see how quickly a difficult situation can deescalate. Children with autism are highly sensitive human beings. If you are anxious or uncertain on the inside, no matter how you smile on the outside, they will feel your anxiety. They can be barometers for your inner life and cannot be fooled! Commit wholeheartedly to your positive intention and positive outcomes will follow. Our thinking, whether positive or negative or all that lies between, can lead to a chain reaction for us and our students like a pinball bouncing its way down through the bumpers.

The Lock: Domino Morning

First, we will present a scenario in which we are locked in our usual way of behaving. We will return to that same scenario but only after going through an exercise to unlock and modify our perception and approach from within.

The following story illustrates the kinds of obstacles that can prevent us from being in the moment with our students and staying true to our intention. Does this sound familiar? You blink to the blurred neon red of your alarm clock. 7:47 AM. The alarm didn't go off and now you are going to be super rushed . . . again.

You spring out of bed and into the shower. No time for conditioner. On the way to work, performance driving like that kid from *Transformers*, you decide to give your usual morning latte a miss. Not a good start. Because you are behind schedule, you lose out on a prime spot in the main lot. As the attendant humorlessly motions you toward the side streets, you think to yourself, give a guy an orange vest and a traffic wand and suddenly he thinks he's king of the world. There are no spaces for what seems like blocks. Of course, this is the day on which your bag is filled with a stack of corrected papers and heavy books rivaling the weight of a full set of *Encyclopaedia Britannica*. Hoisting it like a Nepalese sherpa over your shoulder, the bag handle rips. You scramble, chasing after a blizzard of paper, dozens of essays, and handouts wafting out into the middle of the street. A mother you half-recognize pulls up in her SUV, bumper inches from your head, as you crouch down, frantically collecting papers. Also late for work, the mother honks at you to get out of the way. You stand up, a chaos of papers pressed to your chest, mouth agape.

As you arrive at your desk, the bell rings and children start trickling into class. You have had no prep time; your instant coffee has spilled on your white blouse. Two kids are struggling over another kid's backpack as two others race in amid some game of tag being played at earsplitting decibels. The distractions mount as the classroom escalates into a random cacophony. A small voice inside is pleading with you to regroup and take a "chill pill" before reacting. But that voice isn't loud enough, and before you know it, you are reacting to the energy of the students. The environment of nurturing becomes one of survival, and all the students fall in line to play their starring roles as instigators. The special circumstances of the classroom disappear from your mind-set like a mirage in the desert. Your chest tightens. Your voice rises above the fray. You are yelling now. One child crawls under a table in the far corner where a classroom poster cheerily reads, "One-of-a-Kind Gifts." Your heart sinks. You feel like the most terrible, worst teacher ever. Maybe your mother was right: you should have chosen a more predictable profession—like accounting.

Key One Exercise: Set an Intention

For many teachers, this scenario is not uncommon. Here is an exercise to practice setting an intention that allows you to establish an inner compass that can keep you centered through your day. It is ideal to create a daily ritual at home before coming to the school campus. The first time you do this exercise, it will take about fifteen minutes. Believe me, it's worth it, and once you've done it, you'll find that this process of centering yourself will take only a few minutes. Here goes . . . Find a quiet place where, for a few minutes, you can regroup without distractions. Sit comfortably with your back supported in a chair or on the floor. Get a sense of your body. Plant your sit bones like roots to the chair or floor.

Take a deep breath in and a deep breath out. Close your eyes and get a sense of your body, of the way you are sitting. Feel the way your sit bones are touching the ground or chair. While you are breathing, sense your feet. Move from your feet, up to your calves, then to your thighs. Fill up your chest with air and sense the way your breath moves in and out.

Keep breathing deeply. Get a sense of your shoulders, your back, your arms, your elbows, your wrists, your hands, your fingers. Keep breathing as you get a sense of your neck, the back of your head, your throat, your face, the top of your head. Allow yourself to be fully present in these moments.

Now visualize a golden yellow light that originates from high up in the clouds and that goes down your spine, grounding you to the earth. Let your body be filled with the golden light and breathe in this light. Let it energize your entire body, your muscles, your lungs. Feel your stillness. Now, from this calm place, set your intention for the day. This intention will serve as your reliable compass.

Again, an intention is about your state of being. For example, my intention may be to simply be open. Your intention might be to be playful. So when you find yourself getting a little too serious, you go right back to that intention and see your situation with a sense of playfulness. This may sound difficult but in fact it's a discipline that can be practiced and mastered. You may set an intention to be calm, so when you feel upset, make an effort to return to that feeling of calm.

Breathe into this thought. Give it energy. Visualize yourself placing your intention in your heart. Or, if you're a more practical sort, write it on an index card and carry it with you the entire day. Place the card on your desk or close by. This way, when the day starts unwinding and you need to restore your intention, you'll know where to find it. Never worry if you veer off course. It's not reasonable to expect yourself to always *hold on to* the intention. Just be aware when you're slipping away from it and *return* to the intention as swiftly as you can.

Did you know that when we take a trip in an airplane, our flight is off course more than 90 percent of the time? The guidance system reports to the autopilot that the plane is off course and the autopilot makes the necessary adjustments. This happens thousands of times throughout any given flight. Just as the autopilot adjusts a course, we can make adjustments to get our intention back on course. For on course or off, we need to remember that whatever mood we display—whether positive or negative—the child we are seeking to help will be sure to pick up on it.

The Unlock: It's Never Too Late to Start the Day Over

Now, let's revisit the morning scenario once more, but this time, we'll employ the work we discovered in the exercise of Key One. You still blink to the blurred neon of your alarm clock. Again, you fly out of bed but this time, before you step into the shower, you take a moment. You close your eyes and inhale, directing your breath all the way down toward the base of your spine. You see it there—a glowing ball of peaceful yellow light. Return to the place you discovered in the exercise, that inner place of calm. It may feel counterintuitive to stop and take a long slow breath when you are late and rushed, but it is the most effective way to break the chain of frantic energy. Taking that moment to yourself will make all the difference in how your lateness dictates the ensuing events. "I have all the time in the world . . . to play," you remind yourself. You open your eyes. You set an intention for the day—to be playful. Back in reality, you jump into the shower, shampoo. Speed-racer hair conditioning is followed by the stunt driving and that sorely missed latte, but this time you recall your intention: you have all the time in the world for play.

Losing out on the good parking in the main lot, you succumb to the dictatorial guy in the orange vest and end up a half-mile away from school, nudged between a motorcycle and a fire hydrant. The spring blooms are ablaze and beautiful. It is still the day on which you hoist your overstuffed bag over your shoulder. The handle rips sending dozens of papers flying into the street. As you crouch down, collecting the white carpet of scribbles, you are a near miss for the mother in the SUV. You stand up clutching all your papers, but this time you laugh and she blushes, embarrassed that she almost mowed down a teacher.

You arrive right with the bell and children flooding into class. The two kids are still struggling over another's backpack as another twosome charges in amid the game of tag. The distractions mount to a deafening roar. Again, that tiny voice pleads with you. This time, you realize, it's not too late to start this day over. You step to the middle of the classroom and clear your throat to get every-one's attention. In a Vegas-style boxing match voice, you call out the entangled students names as if prizefighters and do a blow-by-blow radio call of their backpack struggle. The class relaxes and falls into their proper seats to get ready for first period.

As the last stragglers shuffle past you to their seats, you notice that the coffee stain on your blouse is perfectly hidden by the sweater you've thrown over your shoulders. As you head to the front of the class, you remind yourself of your intention. You take your sweater off and ask the students to do something called a Rorschach test, interpreting the "ink" coffee spot. The kids amaze you with their creativity and the level of playfulness rises.

Whether you think you can, or you think you can't—
you're right.

Henry Ford

Meet Special Educator Lisa Johnson

The most effective teachers are the ones who engage with intentions rather than with particular goals. An excellent example is Lisa Johnson. Throughout this book, she will be bringing you insights and stories of her process and successes from the playing field as a teacher.

Elaine met Lisa through a parent who described how Lisa had transformed a special education classroom—one that consisted of fifteen students of all abilities, a very small room, and no resources—into a haven of enthusiastic learners—all surpassing their IEP goals. Lisa developed her skills over time; at the start of her career she was at a loss, perhaps like some of you.

Early in her career, teacher Lisa Johnson, armed with a master's degree in special education, enthusiastically arrived at her first job: to teach children with autism. She had her education, her credentials, ample theoretical training, an arsenal of textbook guidelines, and goals to inspire an imaginary class she had been teaching in her head for years. "Remember to speak slowly. Repeat what you are teaching often. Seat the special education students close to the front of the classroom. Break tasks down into single steps. Simplify the curriculum." She was ready to take on the challenge with these recommendations.

However, she found over time that *some* of these recommendations worked *some* of the time with *some* students, a *few* of them worked *most* of the time with a *few* students, and *none* worked *most* of the time for far too *many*. She felt she was missing the target. No matter how animated she made a lesson, she couldn't hold Sam's attention. Jane wouldn't respond to her questions. Bart seemed lost in his own world and wouldn't even look her in the eye. She had no idea how much of the lesson each was able to absorb, and homework and tests were not reliable indicators given the fine motor challenges and challenged communication skills of her students.

One girl hid under her desk from the overhead lights. Another ran in circles when the chatter around her got too loud. All the tools Lisa implemented had little to no effect. The class was simply not going according to her goals! Some seasoned educators told her, "Don't worry so much; there's only so much a teacher can do. Some kids just can't be taught."

But deep inside, she had a burning belief that there was a better way to support students with severe learning challenges and differences. Although her concrete and quantifiable goal was to get through the textbook material with a B-C grade bell curve, her overarching ambition was to create a room of independent thinkers and self-motivated learners.

Toward this end, she began examining different learning styles. She read educational manuals, met with school psychologists, and tirelessly interviewed every teacher to learn from their experiences. She studied all the certified teaching methodologies and became a conference junkie, picking up different strategies every weekend at airport hotels and taking continuing education credits over the summer. Some things she learned worked for a bit, others flat out failed. Some elevated one student but alienated two others in the process. Determined to a fault, she was not going to stop until she achieved every goal with each student. It took a long time for her to realize that the goal she had set was unattainable. She was on a one-way freeway to frustration and disappointment, and so were her students.

Taking a step in the right direction, she studied and became certified as a DIR graduate (Stanley Greenspan's developmental, individual-difference, relationship-based approach), which focuses on the teacher cultivating a relationship with the student as the necessary foundation for all learning and turns the familiar teacher-as-giver–student-as-receiver paradigm on its head. She immediately had to release her expectations of the daily grind: getting through scheduled curriculum, sticking to semester time lines, and tracking progress graphs. Instead, her focus became how to best connect with her students. Her idea of success in the classroom was no longer measured by test scores or checklists at the end of a chapter. She let go of her *goal* and set an *intention* to be present and truly understanding of her students' differences to reach them in order to teach them. She practiced that intention every day. So can you. Ready. Set. Follow your intention.

From the Trenches

Carol Ishihara, Special Educator

When there is chaos in the classroom, I detach personally from the noise and disruption, unless a student is in danger of being hurt. When I become the "calm within the storm" and stay still and quiet, I find my students reflect that calm. Sometimes I will play classical music such as Mozart.

When Sarah has a meltdown, I quickly ask the aide to take the other students to the library. I give Sarah space to release her energy and tell her that she is safe and that I am staying over at my desk but I am with her. I focus on my breathing and stay calm even as she is raging. Noticing a cup of sharpened pencils and a landmine of backpacks on the floor, I clear away any potential hazards. I monitor her behavior while I pick up a book and read, letting her know that I am aware of her but not obsessed with stopping her. After shrieking and crying in tantrums, she eventually calms down from her emotional escalation. I remain consistent, neither worried by her tantrum nor relieved by her calm. I am her constant through the storm. I gently touch her back, knowing she likes sensory input. Sarah is fatigued, her emotional outrage has exhausted her, and she falls asleep at her desk. The next day, to determine the trigger for the emotional collapse, I take the time to talk to her about what happened. We can find the triggers and bring awareness to them. I find that most emotional outbursts are caused by an unexpected surprise or transition. Simply by being aware of it reduces its power. My intention to remain calm and be an anchor for her allows her to feel safe with me. It validates her emotions and builds a trust between us.

Zack Wimpee, One-on-One Aide

My attitude is that I love all the kids and I try to find the individual differences in all children to give them the best therapy to help them succeed. But at the end of the day, I remember that this is my job, not my life. If you attach yourself too much, you aren't able to let go when work is over. Remaining in good mental and physical health for the kids is very important. You must be able to relax and not bring work home with you in order to recharge and be the best therapist for the next day's work.

Monica Jorgensen, Special Educator

My main strength as an educator is flexibility. It is so important to be able to make plans but more important to let them go if they are not appropriate for that moment. Plans made at home away from the students should never be set in stone. General education teachers have a blueprint for nearly every week of the entire year. They have curriculum outlines and chapter pacing. Because I don't know what kind of progress is going to be made, I try to plan week by week instead. This can become day by day, even minute by minute. My flexibility benefits the kids because a sudden interest that they take on can become a stimulating two-week unit. I take student engagement wherever I find it and run with it.

Three Morning Intentions from Lisa Johnson, Special Educator

First, the door check. Hang up your personal issues before entering the class. Take short breaks throughout the day to clear away any thoughts that may be lingering around. Lisa likes to assure these thoughts that she'll attend to them after school on her own time. She reminds herself that time at school is 100 percent for the students.

Second, be of service. A word that works both ways because you get what you give. The concept of being of service aligns Lisa's principles to her actions. When she begins with an attitude of service, helpfulness is her constant companion. Helpfulness is also contagious to all the students and is a community builder.

Third, remember humor. Lighten up to brighten up. Obviously, there is a time for seriousness in teaching, but adding laughter to a lesson brings a positive charge to the material. A shared laugh is a bonding agent and engages students to participate. Ultimately, we are all seeking joy, and students look forward to being in a classroom infused with the joy of learning.

Quick Keys

- Find your own place of relaxation and peace.

- Set your intention for the day—to be calm, patient, joyful, playful, and so on.

- If you sway from this intention, call on the "autopilot" and readjust.

- Remember that it is never too late to start your day over.

Key Two

Develop Acceptance
and Appreciation

Knowledge of the self is the mother of all knowledge.
So it is incumbent on me to know myself, to know it
completely, to know its minutiae, its characteristics,
its subtleties, and its very atoms.

Kahlil Gibran

Often in our society, people with disabilities are overlooked, marginalized, and not tolerated due to their differences. However, consider this: Abraham Lincoln suffered from severe depression. What if he had been judged and isolated for his social differences and emotional disability? Moses spoke with a lisp. What if no one had listened to him because of his speech issue?

> I was seen as retarded when I was smart, as not under-
> standing when I understood, as lazy when it was impos-
> sibly hard, as narcissistic when I was locked internally.
> *Ido Kedar, fourteen-year-old nonverbal boy with autism*

The fact is, even the people we idolize have qualities that we think of as "defects." No one is perfect and all of us are as individual as snowflakes. We have unique physical and mental attributes. We have particular likes and dislikes: some students like math, others English; some excel at sports, others at art.

Stanley Greenspan always cautioned me [Elaine Hall] to never compare Neal to any other child but only to compare Neal to Neal. I had to see how each year, even though he was not "cured" of his autism or "talking," he was becoming more and more participatory in this world. His body was becoming more regulated and he was becoming more social. Although he remained nonverbal (and still is—even with hundreds of hours of speech therapy), he has learned many ways to communicate: through sign language, typing, icons on his iPod touch, and writing. Had I focused only on the fact that he was not speaking with his mouth, I would have seen only failure and disappointment. By accepting Neal's neurology for what it is, and understanding that he is highly apraxic, which impedes his ability to form sounds with his mouth, I can applaud all of the many ways that Neal does "speak." I can ignore what he isn't and celebrate who he is.

"We all have areas of strengths and weaknesses that create our individual profiles," says Barry Prizant. "Children with autism just have more pronounced strengths and weaknesses. What is the point of judging aspects of our profile as good or bad? It is simply who we are as individuals at the time. We can look at it objectively to determine a natural education plan with supports to continue our personal evolution as a human being."

Key Two allows us to unlock our perceptions of ourselves so that we can become more open and accepting of others.

Educators and parents tend to act
from a "fix-it" mode.

Children with special needs are reminded throughout their day about their *specialness*—a word they tend to view as synonymous with *different*. They are subjected to well-meaning educators and parents, who tend to act from a "fix-it" mode and diligently address children's deficits. If the fact that these special children are considered different slips their minds, they are reminded of it in front of their typical peers, when they are pulled out of class for some form of "fix-it" therapy, whether it's OT, APE, or SL. The student may spend time in a dedicated resource room with other kids who have challenges. These children are constantly reminded of all the things they are not capable of. Outside of school, they have more therapies, doctor's appointments, and myriad treatments. These multiple interventions, although essential, are all attempts to bring the child up to some "acceptable" or "normal" range, but they can also be exhausting and demoralizing, and for those reasons may be counterproductive if not balanced with opportunities for the child to be seen and accepted for exactly who she is *right now*. We are not saying to stop the interventions but rather to be aware of how they may be affecting a child and to make sure there is a balance of work and play in the child's life.

Words are powerful weapons for good or ill and have great impact on all children. Nonverbal children and children with autism in particular are highly sensitive to the meanings that words carry. They are equally sensitive to body language and intonation. It is not what you say but how you say it that has the most influence. Judgment may be implied in a tone or look and may even be unconsciously transmitted. Sometimes well-meaning teachers will talk about a child—in front of the child—as if they weren't there!

Descriptions of a child as "high functioning" or "low functioning" are subjective labels that do not honor the whole person. Each child has different abilities. Sixteen-year-old Neal is nonverbal and would appear "low functioning" in social environments. However, if you hiked with him in the Santa Monica Mountains, he fearlessly leads the group and forges new pathways, and you'd think of him as "high functioning"! Labels are as unreliable as they are limiting. Instead, simply accept all children for exactly who they are.

A man cannot be comfortable without his own approval.

Mark Twain

A Typically "Atypical" Day for Joey

When school is out on Wednesday for Joey, it is just the beginning of his workday. As his mom stresses over the traffic from the rush hour roadwork, Joey has his usual gluten-free snack in the backseat. He is already tired after a long day in class with his one-on-one aide, plus an hour-long session with his OT when he had failed a test because no one could read his printing letters. He had made his best attempt to write in the lines, but even he couldn't read his work. The car hits a deep pothole as it veers off the pavement following a detour, which makes Joey bang his head against the window. He is reminded that he slipped in APE and hit the same spot on the concrete wall. Red lights flash broadcasting yellow signs as a mammoth steamroller rolls by with confidence. Joey closes his eyes to avoid the strobe flash and sees his test paper that was returned after lunch with a lot of red ink on it. As his mom navigates slowly through the maze of road builders, Joey thinks to himself, "Wow. Just like this road, I am always under construction, too."

Of course, there was lovely recess, which he had to spend with gawky plastic cups strapped to the bottoms of his feet that his new occupational therapist is using to help Joey learn to balance himself and feel grounded. As the other fourth-graders play jolly fun handball, Joey clumped around cones on the concrete slalom course. When he lost his focus, he toppled over on his side just as his classmates were returning to class. The kids laughed and Joey laughed, too, trying to act as though the kids were laughing *with* him. Their taunts hurt worse than his hip.

Continuing with his vigorous treatment plan, Joey is en route to SI, then on to SL before making it home to grapple with homework. As Joey gazes out at the world passing him by, he reviews his "unsuccessful" list: the balls he didn't catch, the friends he doesn't have, the papers he can't keep straight, the clothes he didn't keep clean.

Joey doesn't care for Wednesdays.

The Key to Accepting Others Starts with Accepting and Appreciating Yourself

Years of habitual "if only . . ." thinking sets us up to focus on what's wrong with ourselves and makes it harder to recognize the many things we do that are effective and positive.

> I have not failed. I have just found 10,000 ways that won't work.
>
> *Thomas Edison*

Key Two is a tool that will help you to know, accept, and love yourself as you are. It abolishes criteria against which you measure whether or not you are worthy or have done enough. That is a losing game and, like the house in Vegas, it simply can't be beat.

The Lock: The Up-Down

You're approaching the end of the school day. The kids are all tired by the time you get them for fifth period, but no one is more tired than Cyrus, one of the kids mainstreamed into your class. You want to be compassionate and open to his needs, but nothing you ever do works with him and his constant physical motion just drives you crazy. You feel as though he hasn't heard a word you've said all year. Other members of the support team talk about how amazing he is but somehow you feel like nothing you do is ever good enough for this kid. Nor will it be.

As you enter the class, Cyrus is already there with his aide, Raphael. You say hello and try to snatch a moment of eye contact, but the neatly dressed, messy-haired kid isn't interested. He rocks back and forth staring at a spot on the floor located somewhere just beyond your left ankle. The bell clangs and the students amble into class. You begin the lesson, asking one of the students to read aloud from your favorite Dickens novel, A *Tale of Two Cities*. As she does, Cyrus begins what you have come to call "the up-down." It's a distracting motion of getting up and sitting back down at random times throughout the entire period. You've tried numerous strategies for addressing this disruptive activity: moving students who are easily distracted; moving Cyrus to the back, front, and side of the room; and even changing out his desk for a separate table and chair.

The student who is reading from the novel falters, distracted by Cyrus's movements. You look to the aide who tries to intervene but to no avail. You pause the reading and directly address Cyrus. He continues the up-down. You try again, frustration mounting. "We're not doing this right now, Cyrus," you firmly say. "Do you see how everyone around you is listening?"

The aide senses your impatience—as do all the students. "We're going to take a break," the aide softly tells you. He whispers to Cyrus, who takes his arm. Defeated, you watch them exit. How do you learn to accept this? How can you ask other students to ignore it when it's so distracting to you? But then, you stop to wonder, why does it annoy you so much?

Key Two Exercise: I Am . . .

Key Two allows us to unlock our perceptions of ourselves and thereby accept others. Let's start with an exercise. Take ten minutes, three pieces of paper, and a pencil or pen. On the first piece of paper, write down three things that you are not good at.

For example, "I am not good at organizing papers" or "I am not a good cook" or "I have trouble with mathematics." If you are doing this exercise with a partner, switch papers and ask him or her to read out loud to you and replace the word *I* with *you*. (For example, "You are not good at organizing. You are not a good cook. You are bad at math.") If you are doing the exercise alone, read it out loud, imagining that you are talking to yourself as a child. Sense how it makes you *feel* to hear these words directed back at you. Now think how many times a day you may say these things to yourself! How often do you criticize yourself and tell yourself that you are not enough? Five times a day? Ten times? Twenty times or more? When we do this in a large workshop we learn that nearly 75 percent of the people present tell themselves negative things constantly throughout their day. We are going to give you permission right now, today, to stop doing this!

Now, think about how many times a day our kids with special needs hear about what is wrong with them. "He can't talk; she needs help with vowels; he can't write; she doesn't know her times tables; he can't stay in his chair." Talking to other adults in front of the child with special needs, describing their deficits, often happens in front of nonverbal children with autism. Remember just because a child cannot speak does not mean he cannot hear and feel your comments!

Let's take this one step further. Imagine if you were in an environment where you had to use your deficits all day and were constantly reminded what you were not capable of. For example, it is easier for Elaine to write a script or a story than to make copies of it and collate it. Now imagine if all day long in school, she had to copy and collate paper before she was permitted to write. By the time she got to writing, she'd not only be exhausted but also frustrated. Sure, she might get good at collating—but at what cost? Or take the example of Diane, who's a world-class athlete. She doesn't like to sit very long. She needs to get up, move around, sit on the floor, stretch. What if she were judged more on her inability to sit still than on her amazing physical prowess?

Although most of us can easily rattle off a laundry list of things that we are not good at or things that we can't do or haven't done, all too often we are hard-pressed to acknowledge our attributes. Perhaps culturally, we have been taught not to brag, that self-denigration is somehow more acceptable, humble, and polite. At the same time, we live in a world that insists that we achieve and set our sights high even as we judge ourselves for not doing or being enough. We live in a judgmental society, and the people we are hardest on are ourselves.

Stop telling yourself what is wrong with you! Stop the self-judgment and criticism. Take a moment and see where and when these negative thoughts began. Whose "voice" is telling you these things? We can't change or undo the past, but we can create new voices in our heads, voices that comfort and guide rather than criticize and demean. Which brings us to the second part of this exercise.

Take the second piece of paper and write down three positive things about yourself. Sure, this isn't easy. But if we don't know and love ourselves for who we are, who will? Start with something easy such as "I'm a good listener" or "I'm a good friend." Then go bold with "I am extremely creative. I have beautiful eyes." Give this paper to your partner or read it out loud as if you were talking to yourself as a child and replace the *I* with *you*. How does this feel? Pretty nice, yes? In our workshops both those receiving the positive words and those giving the positive words feel happier and more energized.

Now imagine if each time you saw your students who have special needs, you pointed out something positive about them. Imagine how that would make them feel when they are trying so desperately to float in a sea that constantly threatens to engulf them. What if you were the one person during the school day who pointed out, "Wow, I love how gentle you are when holding the hamster" or "I love when you look at me and listen so well for directions."

You will become a safe port for these students. You will be someone they can trust and open up to. The more you find things to praise in these students, the more you'll find that their deficits decrease.

Imagine if a child walks into an environment in which he is completely accepted and honored for everything he is. He is not looked at as "a work in progress" and is welcomed into a community that respects his differences. She is not viewed as impaired or in need of help. Imagine how empowering it is for these children to see that others believe that they are uniquely whole and perfect exactly as they are. This is how children are met at The Miracle Project.

Now for the final part of this exercise. Take a moment and return to that calm space from Key One. Look inside and just *be* with your breath. *Be* with yourself. Nothing positive, nothing negative, just being. Imagine putting your arm around yourself as a small child and loving and accepting yourself for exactly who you are. Breathe into this feeling and slowly open your eyes.

Jot down on the third piece of paper how this last exercise made you feel. It might bring up sadness, as few of us have had that much-desired experience of being unconditionally loved and appreciated for exactly who we are. You may want to return to this part of the exercise often. You may also want to keep a list of all of your own positive attributes. And always remember: we are not perfect humans; we are perfectly human.

The Unlock: Turning the Down to Up

Now, armed with our newly found self-acceptance, let's return to school. When the school day ends, you attend a staff meeting. Much of it is boilerplate school business: logistics, fire drills, and state testing. You always doodle in these mandatory meetings, decorating the edges of the same old handouts and reviewing your internal checklist. The meeting leader is Clifford Powers, the vice principal who has a way of calling people out as if to prove something. As your doodling reminds you to e-mail the class newsletter, you hear your name spoken.

"Ms. Worthingon, I see we have an artist in the midst," he mocks your doodling. "Please pay attention! This is important information. Or would you like to share your little masterpiece with the rest of the staff?"

You redden, embarrassed and feeling that familiar sense of unease, as if you are ten years old and being called to the principal's office. You start to beat yourself up, berating yourself for daydreaming, wishing you could pay better attention. Like Cyrus, you have trouble holding focus and sitting still. You multitask and find it incredibly difficult to hold your focus on any one thing. You beat yourself up about this all the time. You are, after all, an educated teacher and should be able to maintain mental discipline, but all too often your brain goes here, then there, then over to yet another flying thought, like a flurry of balls in a ping-pong match.

However, this time you brace yourself and stop the self-flagellation. Armed with self-love and acceptance, you stand up for yourself as you have always stood up for others. "Mr. Powers," you say, "I am and was listening; actually, drawing helps me pay attention in these long meetings."

You repeat to Mr. Powers exactly what he said while you were doodling. It's an "aha!" moment—for what you just acknowledged about yourself gives you insight into Cyrus. He may not *seem* like he is listening, but then again, you certainly didn't appear to be either. A connection is made!

The next day during reading class, Cyrus takes his seat and as soon as another child begins to read from the book, he begins his up-down ritual. When the chapter is done, you ask Cyrus to share with the class what was just read. He continues playing with his string, while he explains the theme of Chapter One even using verbatim quotes from the book: "It was the best of times and it was the worst of times . . ." Through all of his distracting behaviors, he had been listening. Once you accepted his behavior and didn't try to manage, control, or judge him, he was able to show you what he actually knew. The actions that you perceive as Cyrus's way to not be present in class are the very coping mechanisms that allow him to be attentive and learn. Just like your doodling helps you to stay focused. This is your introduction to understanding the unique process that Cyrus uses to absorb the world and an invitation to understand your own process as well as that of other students. Removing conditions and judgments is a direct way into the minds and hearts of students.

> Neither a lofty degree of intelligence, nor imagination, nor both together, go to the making of genius. Love, love, love. That is the soul of genius.
>
> *Wolfgang Amadeus Mozart*

It is important to note that this is not a "magical" fix. Not every child will respond to this approach 100 percent of the time. Huge gains may not always be made. But incremental progress is constantly achieved when you approach another human being with acceptance, compassion, and understanding.

Even if the child does not progress in her outward ability, think of the gift you are giving her by accepting her individual differences, by not judging her and allowing her own process to unfold. Think of the gift you are giving yourself by being in a loving emotional state.

Many times growth and progress take time to show results. Elaine tells a story in her book, *Now I See the Moon*, about a man so eager to "help" a butterfly that he opens its chrysalis too soon. The result is that the butterfly's wings never properly develop and the butterfly cannot ever fly. Growth takes time. We may not always see the internal changes just as we do not witness the hidden development of the butterfly's wings. Elaine has children who come to her classes for weeks or even months and do nothing more than sit and watch class. She accepts them for exactly who they are and allows them to sit until they are ready to participate. In time, these same students are singing songs, dancing, and becoming a vital part of the class. Had she tried to coerce or force their participation, they may have never participated.

You may never see a particular child's metamorphosis. It may occur long after he is gone from your classroom. But know you are planting the seeds for his development by creating a positive relationship and nurturing atmosphere. Let's take this one step closer to you because ultimately, we have control only over our own growth and development. How do *you* feel when you appreciate and accept others for who and where they are? It feels good, yes? Perhaps that good feeling can carry over during challenging times and provide you with an ongoing source of nurturance and energy. True vision begins with seeing yourself completely and extends to perceiving others more accurately.

From the Trenches

Carol Ishihara, Special Educator

I truly see all my students for their strengths once I can see my own strengths. If I can facilitate students in ferreting out what it is that they really enjoy and are good at and focus on that, the students will see themselves as class experts in that area. I call this "keeping their eye on the prize." I am open to handing out expert nomenclature if I feel ownership of the expert in me. I acknowledge my aptitude in listening and observing without judging each and every student. From that place of wonder, I see their uniqueness and crown it with a title. I like to give all students a special title based on what they determine as their area of strength, such as "Mr. Fix It," "Resident Actor," or "Mad Scientist." If they have confidence in their field, they are able to reach outside that realm with the same confidence and try new subjects, thereby expanding their knowledge base. When students are viewed by their peers as an authority in a certain area, their self-esteem flourishes and they are more apt to participate and lead throughout the class. The essential part is that I must first honor the expert, and sometimes experts, within myself.

Lisa Johnson's Tale of Acceptance and Understanding

Lisa Johnson's first job as a special education teacher was to take over an "out-of-control" class. The current teacher, Mr. R, was a long-term substitute for this notoriously wild group of special needs kids, and he was making a rapid exit on Friday. The school did not wish to share the (ugly) details of his difficult tenure with a bright-eyed new graduate like her. Before the end of the week, she visited the class for half a day to make observations about what was—and wasn't—working to help design the new structure of the classroom and revise the curriculum delivery style. Because the present situation was not good, she didn't want to repeat the same mistakes.

Sitting in the back of the class, the students were immediately interested in this strange visitor. They stared and asked her questions. "Are you here to watch him or us? Are you someone's parent?" Mr. R was quick to reprimand their behavior but not before she noted that the students were engaging and friendly. When Mr. R turned his back, the students joked with each other. He tried to curb their banter, so they asked questions that they clearly knew the answers to, making strange noises and letting him know they—and not he—were in control. In this chaos, Lisa noticed that they all had a sense of humor.

Mr. R tells told her he was merely helping out and that he had a "real" job elsewhere. He spoke loudly in front of the students about this personal fact and how teaching wasn't really his thing. In turn, the students knew that Mr. R was not serious about being there; therefore, they were not serious about learning. After lunch Mr. R literally fell asleep on a drafting table he used as his desk and, apparently, as his pillow. Imagine how the kids must have felt. No wonder they ridiculed the teacher and were labeled "out of control." They had every right to live up to that moniker. The teacher was dead asleep!

Lisa began her work in the classroom by transforming the space, removing random posters to reduce the visual clutter and getting rid of the drafting board desk because it was a reminder of Mr. R's snoozing perch. She rearranged all the desks in a circle, creating a community-style setting. Now, the students could look at each other instead of seeing the backs of heads.

Now for the tricky construction of building a trusting relationship with these students. She already knew these students were lively, interesting, funny, and spirited, whereas the school saw only their disrespectful and undisciplined behavior. The students had years of a naughty reputation to uphold, so at first, the teacher transition was barely acknowledged. The students had been so in their own world for years of school that they didn't know about discipline, rules, and foundational tasks such as note taking, lectures, homework, and so on. The students used their crude humor to avoid academics and waste time, so Lisa simply listened to them.

She started to write down their dialogue and jokes. She then wrote on the board "What's Your Story?" She asked them to write various dialogue scenes that would tell about their lives, their dreams, their likes and dislikes. She wrote a character for herself.

Using their own words, they cobbled together a few scenes and got ready to perform it. Lisa dimmed the lights and drew a poster on the chalkboard promoting the play. Each student did his or her funny and poignant story on the classroom stage. Lisa listened and learned so much about her students and then shared her story so they could know a personal part of her. It was a bonding experience that created a common trust and respect for each other.

Lisa set up a point system for all positive actions, without penalties for nonpositive behaviors, so they could earn tangible accomplishments. With a quick redo of the room physically, she cleared out the patterns of the past and created a dynamic and fun learning environment going forward. In a few weeks, the students bonded and had new insight into all of the other unique individuals in the classroom.

> Put the magnifying glass down and see the child as a
> child, not as a bunch of weaknesses.
>
> *Anonymous Parent*

Diane's Story of Acceptance

Groundhog Day 2001 was the day my son Wyatt was diagnosed with autism. He was already six years old and had confused the medical community with his unique combination of an outgoing personality and inherent challenges such as tying shoes or playing with peers. He was self-sufficient: a wooden spoon or a flower could keep him engaged for hours. However, he needed support and prompts to self-care such as getting dressed (with the labels on the back and inside), choosing weather-appropriate clothes, towel drying after a bath, and chewing his pasta before swallowing it whole. He was 6 going on 2 on some levels and 6 going on 106 given his surprising wisdom and Buddhalike acceptance and calm.

Wyatt would rise every morning with a smile on his face. He was innately content, nonmaterialistic, noncompetitive, and caring. He was affectionate and loved to laugh. However, he was "failing to thrive" according to the pediatric milestone chart as well as on academic standards; had unpredictable sensory sensitivities to sound, light, and smell; and often seemed to drift off into space. We'd been through years of tests attempting to diagnose the cause of his macrocephaly (large head size) and hypotonia (low muscle tone). He also had problems with fine and gross motor planning: his handwriting was an uncontrolled scribble and he couldn't run or balance on one leg.

Typically, autism is diagnosed before the age of three, but because Wyatt did not have the textbook behaviors of autism, we danced around other diagnoses until one day, enough was enough. The groundhog saw his shadow and Wyatt was officially on the "spectrum."

And suddenly, so was I. The diagnosis was not easy to accept. Like all troubling news in life, it required transitioning through the seven stages of grief:

1. The initial shock and denial ("Maybe they got it wrong . . .").

2. Moving into the deep pain of blaming oneself ("What did I do to cause this?"), which develops into

3. Anger ("Why me, damn it?"), landing in

4. Depression and feelings of isolation ("I am so alone in this.").

These natural stages are essential to healing and come and go in their own time. They can be passed through overnight or they can take years. But, one way or another, you finally reach the three final stages:

5. The upward turn and renewed perspective ("It is not devastating after all.").

6. Reconstruction and working through ("Let's try these possible solutions.") to arrive at

7. Acceptance and hope ("There can be joy here.").

I knew intellectually to move rapidly through stages one through four and thought I worked through them all in record time. Yet in retrospect, I realize I was fumbling on the first stage! I was stuck at, "They most probably—okay, *definitely*—got it wrong!"

I suppressed the label *autism,* hiding it from others and even from myself. I never spoke about "it" and didn't even tell my parents or sisters for quite some time. I had autism wrapped up in a tidy package that I peeked at occasionally through a small opening. I felt that if I just didn't open it, the contents of the package could potentially change. Maybe it wouldn't be autism come Christmas morning. I was dancing with denial.

I also avoided that serious moment of truth with Wyatt, so *autism* was a word he had barely heard. I made sure that he didn't see the file of his tests, IEP, or the copious articles about autism that I was accumulating. I made sure that he didn't hear the doctor talk about his autism and that he didn't know why he was being subjected to all these tests. I told myself that autism was a label that I would navigate privately and that he didn't need to carry the baggage of autism around in him. Now I realize that I didn't make it an official part of Wyatt's life because I didn't want to make it an official part of *my* life. In my determination to be "normal," autism was a "bad" word. To me. Which, as I now realize, made it a bad word to Wyatt. I thought I was protecting him from this unwanted truth, when in fact, I was protecting myself while propagating this lie of omission. It was the wrong tactic, especially given the fact that early intervention is critical.

When it came to school and therapies, I used the term *special needs*, which felt more forgiving, ambiguous, and noncommittal in its diagnosis. Plus, *special* is a positive, complimentary adjective. I could say *special needs* with ease; I could repeat this to my family and friends. It didn't feel as condemning as *autism*. After all, as Wyatt says, "We *all* have special needs."

So Wyatt and I began our "special" journey together. As the parent of a typically developing son named Jackson, Wyatt's older brother, I had already experienced the desire do virtually anything for my child's well-being. When autism raised the stakes, I embarked on an amplified mission to find ways to help Wyatt. I spent hours on the web, in bookstores, scanning medical journals. Even though I really didn't accept the label of *autism*, I needed to know everything about it. It was a full-time job. I discovered, like most parents grappling with a diagnosis, that autism requires unlimited time, resources, and perseverance.

For five years, Wyatt attended adult-led therapy sessions to "fix" his deficits. He needed help with fine and gross motor functions, speech and language, sensory integration, socialization, and self-expression. He developed relationships with his one-on-one therapists but connecting with his peers remained a challenge. So Wyatt attended social skills classes to learn how to make friends. He was taught to shake hands to say hello, to participate in group games, and make a playdate on the telephone, but these procedures seemed to fade away after the class ran its course. Although they made total sense to me, they were not natural fits for Wyatt. He retreated into himself and spent more time in his imagination with his inner-world friends. He preferred those friends because, as he said, "they cannot hurt me." Even with all the external efforts Wyatt was withdrawing.

Due to our overbooked schedule of therapies and the fact that Wyatt's differences made other kids and their moms uncomfortable, Wyatt and I were invited to fewer and fewer playdates. There was little basis for connection. Wyatt couldn't keep up with the fast motoring of typical kids so sports were out, and he had his own style of play that most kids didn't share. Soon, we were off the invitation lists altogether.

Wyatt had fewer and fewer friends. I had fewer and fewer mommy friends. We had lost our connection with the typical community and, because we weren't committing to the world of autism, we hadn't cultivated new relationships with families living with autism. We were lonely when we most needed a social network. I could claim we were victims of a harsh, judgmental society, but in actuality, I created that separation. It would take some time but we would forge a path to a community. It is our human nature to be part of a tribe. The trouble was, I was having difficulty accepting which tribe we belonged to.

This feeling of isolation translated to Wyatt's academic life. Starting in fifth grade, after years of being in a special needs classroom, Wyatt was determined to mainstream in as many subjects as possible. He felt that if he could prove to his peers that he could keep up with them in a class like history, his special needs would disappear and he would be accepted by the typical fifth-graders. He was self-motivated and determined and soon was mainstreaming daily in a variety of subjects. I can only imagine the courage it took to walk across the concrete yard from his special needs annex and enter the main elementary building to drop in on a class already in progress and filled with kids who'd been together since homeroom. He was an outsider on many levels and intent on overcoming his separation and joining ranks with his peers. We often overheard him talking to himself about this magical classroom that he was a part of. He fantasized that the most popular kids were his new best friends, a dream that grew to the point of obsession. It was his sheer desire to be considered "normal," or at the very least to not be "special."

It was a dream destined to not come true: his classmates, typically developing fifth-graders, were at a stage in life when kids aren't particularly accepting of differences. Here comes Wyatt with his open heart and unfiltered smile and they're laughing at him because he's wearing what is—in their view—the wrong color of sneakers. The typical kids would tolerate his presence in their class under the watch of the teacher but during social time and on the playground he became invisible to them. He forged ahead but the stress outweighed the benefits. He developed severe anxiety and was literally grinding down his front teeth. He was often completely switched off, his bright personality dulled to a flat gray. This wasn't my colorful son. He was caught between two worlds and both felt alien to him. Now, he was experiencing the same scenario at school that I had created at home. He was trying to be something he wasn't to please kids he could never please, while trying not to be something that he was: a kid with special needs.

At an emergency IEP I decided to check out a nonpublic school that was specifically for children on the autism spectrum. I had looked at it before and had quickly decided that it wasn't for us. I had limited vision, witnessing students' behaviors, while missing the way teachers were skillfully supporting each student. I saw the individual differences, rather than a rich, diverse community. This time around, I vowed to look without preconceived ideas to choose the best option for Wyatt for this necessary transition. Its nurturing learning environment was an obvious fit for Wyatt. The sixth-grade classroom was interactive and refreshing, with a creative teacher and curious students engaging in discussions. I could hear Wyatt contributing his thoughts as a valued part of a dynamic classroom. I could see him at lunch with other kids, in the center of a community rather than the kid on the outside looking in.

> People are always looking for the single magic bullet that will totally change everything. There is no single magic bullet.
>
> *Temple Grandin*

Yet even enrolling in this school, I still dreamed about discovering a hidden protocol that would miraculously transform my son to normal and send him back into mainstream classes with his head held high. I envisioned telling everyone about some powerful herb, revolutionary diet, or electromagnetic stimulation that had instantly removed his special needs. I remember reading stories of kids overcoming cancer or terrible accidents. I thought that Wyatt would be the exception to the rule and overcome autism. I had scripted the happy ending of our dramatic story all the way to being "normal." Wyatt could show the mainstream kids he's just like them. But was he determined to be normal or was that my agenda? I was the one navigating around autism instead of accepting it and accepting Wyatt for all of his uniqueness. At The Help Group, Wyatt expresses what makes him special and extraordinary. He tells me, "Normal is actually overrated!"

Quick Keys

- Find your own self-acceptance.

- Look for the abilities within each child.

- Keep a list of what each student can do.

- Remember that everyone has special needs.

Key Three

Understand Sensory Profile

Experience is the teacher of all things.

Julius Caesar

We experience the world through our senses. Our senses give us the ability to touch, taste, smell, hear, and see. Most children with autism process and interpret senses differently than their typically developing peers. Some children with autism have difficulty distinguishing between background noise and a person talking to them, or distinguishing between auditory and visual input. Sounds can be too loud or visuals too bright at any moment. Similarly, touch can be a factor with autism. Even seemingly soft things can feel itchy or irritating to hypersensitive skin. Certain smells can become overbearing. The unpredictability of the world can cause anxiety and overwhelm, causing outbursts and a lack of body control. A child may retreat in an attempt to avoid the stimuli and to protect a sensory profile that is delicate and supersensitive.

Temple Grandin, an adult with autism who is a best-selling author, doctor of animal science, and professor at Colorado State University, has developed an acute sensitivity and understanding of animal behaviors. She has compared her auditory input at times to be like a tooth being drilled. One boy named Jasper can hear a jet at 32,000 feet away, long before others, but if a car's brake pad squeals, he may fall into convulsions from the intense inner ear pain. Most often, sensory input is received imbalanced and can be a gross distraction for the child.

Professor and international speaker Stephen Shore understands through his own autism how a barrage of external stimuli can overwhelm the senses:

> I have difficulty separating foreground from background sounds. The noises coming from outside the window—such as a lawnmower, a car, a siren—and the sounds from within the classroom—like the fan in the projector, the scratching of students' pencils on paper during a test, the clock, and period bell—everything entered my auditory processing with equal volume as if I had all the channels of the TV on at once. Obviously I was unable to decipher the words of the teacher with this cacophony of distractions. This also led to behaviors to avoid this auditory assault.

Tito Mukhopadhyay is an extraordinary young man from South India who is autistic and nonverbal. Tito is a prolific writer and has written beautiful works of poetry and authored several books that describe his inner experiences having autism. He explains how he processes the world in his book *How Can I Talk If My Lips Don't Move?*

> If I am in a garden, where there is a garden tap, and water is filling up a red bucket, which is a dynamic situation, changing from instant to instant, I first notice the color of the bucket. I might easily get distracted by its redness, since it could remind me of how my hands bled when I had fallen from a swing, how I was so absorbed in that red that I had forgotten about my pain, and how that red resembled a hibiscus . . .

I would then realize that I was hearing the sound of the water, wondering why that sound reminded me of a drowning man's last blood flow, although I had never seen a drowning man in real life, let alone the flow of his blood . . .

The bucket is filled up eventually, and I see water spilling from it. I understand the situation, waking from my branching thoughts, summing up the components into one conclusion, which is "water filling up a bucket from a garden tap."

Often you will see children with autism exhibiting what may appear to be odd behaviors, such as hand flapping and rocking back and forth. These can actually be coping mechanisms to manage external stimuli. We all do things to calm our bodies. We may twirl our hair, shake our foot while sitting, doodle, or daydream; similarly someone with autism may spin or even, seemingly paradoxically, bang his head against a wall. The key is to discern what the behavior is communicating at its core. An OT can help you identify what sensory needs your students may have and show you how to supply those needs in appropriate ways.

When you see a child screaming, he may be reacting to something that you are not even aware of. If you see a child move her body in way that she has absolutely no control over, disciplinary actions do not work. They are senseless. Often, children with autism cannot control the ways that their bodies react, and believe me, it troubles them more than it troubles you. On Neal's fourteenth birthday, I asked him what he wished for. He typed, "I pray for my body to be still."

Because these outward behaviors often result from overstimulation or disregulation, the stimulus causing them may not be apparent to people who do not have such hypersensitivities. Florescent lights can be a terrible distraction to a child with autism who has described them as "sharp arrows shooting down on my head" or "the way popcorn must feel in the microwave." The buzz these lights generate blends into the room tone for most but can pierce the sensitive ears of those on the spectrum and actually cause pain to a child, like a stabbing in the brain. It's similar to the way in which a dog can pick up an otherwise inaudible frequency that sends him into erratic and unpredictable behaviors. Without proper filtering, any environment can be a minefield for a hyper-sensitive being. A clock's ticking can drown out all other input and make classroom instruction impossible to absorb.

Because tactile experiences can be exaggerated in a child with autism, you may need to be mindful when you do art projects that call for sticky glue, gooey paint, rough paper, or clay. You may want to ask your OT to introduce new tactile sensations in private OT sessions.

Dr. Ricki Robinson, author of the groundbreaking book *Autism Solutions* (Harlequin, 2011), writes that "the inability to process sensory information—either misinterpreting the input or having a delayed response—is what happens to children with ASD all day long."

It is critical to scan the environment for potential stimulation that may create sensory disturbances for children in the classroom. Sitting by the window may seem like a nice idea, but if there is playground activity or a road nearby, the child may be drawn into that distracting outside world. Some children can hear through walls and across rooms and struggle to filter out the multitude of sounds. It is challenging to listen to one conversation in front of you if there is another one happening behind you and it is heard at equal volume. Visual perception can be thrown off when both the foreground and the background are competing for the mind's focus. It becomes a wrestling match within what is being perceived, and often the child cocoons herself to avoid such conflict.

Obviously, it is impossible to provide perfect peace and quiet for one child in an active classroom. The point is not to control the environment to an unnatural point but to develop an awareness about the possible distractions for particular children, most of which can be avoided with simple variations and adjustments. Alternative lighting can be used or direct overhead fluorescent bars turned off, both of which make a difference without changing the overall dynamic of a classroom. The child with autism is in a mainstream classroom to integrate, and you should not feel called on to create a sterile, overprotective environment. You may suggest that a child who is very sensitive to sound wear earphones or ear plugs when things get too loud. Mostly, allow yourself to be conscious and sensitive to sensory stimulus and the way it may affect a child.

Ido Kedar, a fourteen-year-old with autism, expresses his sensory challenges in any given environment:

> My senses are strong. I can hear through walls and across rooms. I have to struggle to filter out the multitude of sounds I hear. You intuitively know what sound is important. This is lucky because I can't. The air conditioner, the dog bark, the conversation, the fridge hum are all equal in my mind. When I was little it was too much information. It overwhelmed so much I would tune out and stim. I have learned to concentrate on speech, but if there are two or more conversations at the same time, I am struggling to keep on one and it's hard. For example, in a restaurant or a dinner party the hum of the voices is like a loud horrible Babel to me. Visually too I get overwhelmed. It's as if I see everything foreground and nothing in the background. Sometimes I see in a tunnel and I miss the sides. Other times I see the sides and miss the big picture because I'm lost in details.

Each child has his or her own ways and sensory thresholds, so observe the individual reactions of each child and make whatever adjustments you can reasonably make to keep the classroom in harmony. Often children can overcome adverse reactions if you support them, reassure them, and walk them through the experience.

Children with autism are known to have difficulties with transitions from one activity or venue to another. Yet the culprit is not the transition itself but rather the fear of what type of sensory assault may occur in an unknown environment. You can prepare children for these transitions by showing them pictures of new spaces, acknowledging their sensory sensitivities, and letting them know what they can expect in the environment they will be entering.

> Autism itself is not the enemy . . . the barriers to development that are included with autism are the enemy. The sensory problems that are often themselves the barriers are the enemy. These things are not part of who the child is . . . they are barriers to who the child is meant to be. Work with the child's strengths to overcome the weaknesses, and work within the autism, not against it, to overcome the developmental barriers.
>
> Frank Klein, *adult with autism and autism advocate*

Sometimes extreme sensitivity has benefits. Children with auditory sensitivity may also have perfect pitch and can sing and play instruments; children with extraordinary visual sense may have great visual memories and excel with computers, maps, or geography. During the exercise later in this chapter, you will observe your sensory profile and experience what sets off your sensory overload. This will allow you to journey into the inner world of autism. But first, let's check into a typical lunchroom in a typical elementary school.

The Lock: Food Fight

Here's a familiar but hypothetical scenario in which a teacher fails to understand the delicate sensory profile of a child with autism:

Let's imagine you are a teacher assigned to lunch patrol and you enter the lion's den of institutional culinary mayhem. The acoustics have never been great in the high-ceiling lunch hall but today it is raining outside and the room is especially chaotic.

A group of six kids is holding a boisterous conversation at the center table, while another gaggle rehearses a rap act in a far corner. Behind the counter, a cafeteria attendant runs a loud industrial mixer to finish off a second batch of mashed potatoes. An oven alarm dings. Then, there is a crash from the lunch line. A student has dropped his tray, sending runny food pooling everywhere. Kids back out of the way, and there's a wave of guffawing mockery from all around the student who dropped the tray. He smiles and takes a bow.

Scanning the room for anything or anyone who needs attention, you spot Carson in the corner. He's not one of your students, but you're aware that he has "behavioral issues" related to ASD. Carson rocks back and forth next to his aide, making loud unintelligible bleating noises and kicking hard at the floor, knees banging under the table. His hands fly as they send vegetables and bits of gravy and potato into the walls. Irritated, other kids move away from him as you cross to intervene.

Girl student (pulling a green bean from her hair): Cut it out, Carson! You're so disgusting!

A colleague teacher also on lunch patrol (shouting to be heard over the entire scene): Hey! Carson! Buddy! No throwing your lunch!

Carson thrashes even more violently. No eye contact. His aide shakes his head and signals that this isn't the way to calm his student down.

You observe all the pandemonium and start to feel stressed because you want to do something to take control of the situation. Because you are on lunch patrol and need to follow through with your responsibilities, you ignore the aide, support the other lunch patroller, and move in closer and yell loudly, "Hey, you're going to stop this behavior right now!! We don't kick the tables and throw! Is this the way you act at home?!"

Before you can finish, Carson hurls the tray at the other teacher. It clangs on the floor. Gravy, potatoes, and butterscotch pudding run down his shirt in a colorful splatter that rivals a Jackson Pollack painting.

You are taken aback by the sudden silence of the packed cafeteria as the kids survey the damage. Your colleague brews to a robust red and gets up slowly. A rousing cheer wells up from behind the soggy teacher in support of Carson. The bell sounds the end of Round One. You can't help but wonder if there might have been a better way to handle the situation.

Key Three Exercise: The Inside Job

Before we revisit the lunch room calamity, let's take some time away and get to know our own sensory system. The following is a guided meditation. You may first want to read it through or read it into a recording device and play it back so that you can be more fully involved in the exercise.

Sit on the floor. Take off your shoes. Go into your inner space and clear your mind. Take some deep breaths and let everything go. We are going to journey into the five senses, first observing your sensory checklist, then taking it to levels that many children with autism experience.

Listen to the *sounds* around you. Close your eyes. Listen to the sounds inside your own body. Now, start to increase the volume on the sounds—become one giant sound machine—let there be nothing but sound and let all the sounds become exaggerated!

Have it build to a crescendo; tune into how you feel. Take a deep breath and let that go.

Open your eyes and look at the room around you like you are looking at it for the very first time. Take notice of all the things in your field of vision: lights, colors, textures, movement. Now start to imagine that the lights become brighter, the colors ignite, and things in motion accelerate as though your eyes are barraged with color and form. Take that experience in. Close your eyes and erase the vision field.

Turn your focus now to touch. Start to feel your clothes, your skin, the carpet, or an object. Notice the textures, the many sensations that are right at your fingertips. Start to imagine that what you are touching is like sandpaper, rough, irritating to the senses. The clothes you wear are itchy. Let that overtake you. Now let that go.

Turn your focus to your tongue. Taste what is happening inside your mouth. Imagine sweet, sour, pungent, metallic, acid, bitter— amplify the tastes and notice how they can consume you. Now let that go.

Smell what is happening around you—your hands, your clothes, the air. Breathe in deeply and notice the many smell sensations. Let those scents build to a point where they fill you up. Good smells, bad smells, a dumpster, a rotten egg, a flower, low tide. Let all these smells blend into one huge sensory experience. Now close off the smell.

From an empty space inside, let's put all five senses into action: First, hearing, let all the sounds come in. Keep that going and add touch, a need to touch everything around you. Continue being sensitive to sounds and touch and now add taste, smell, and visuals. Imagine that each sense is fighting to be the most noticed. Let the war of the senses build. Let everything become heightened and out of control. Let your senses consume you. Now try and think about anything else except what is happening in your sensory experience. Try to have a conversation while all this internal chaos is going on. You can't. Welcome to autism!

Tune into how you were feeling when all of your senses were heightened. Anxious? Overwhelmed? Every time Elaine does this exercise at workshops she hears the same responses from the audience: "I felt anxious, overwhelmed. I did not want to be social; I wanted to retreat; I couldn't focus. I felt isolated. It was hard to breathe." These words create a perfect description of what it feels like to have autism.

For the next week, let yourself be acutely aware of your senses. Pay attention to little noises that might irritate you or the kinds of clothing that cause discomfort. Start to catalog where you have sensory sensitivity. We all do! A ticking clock reminds Elaine of the crocodile in *Peter Pan!* She can't concentrate when a clock is too loud and can't sleep if there is even a muffled ticking in the room. What sense makes you "tick" or send you over the edge?

The Unlock: Food Peace

Now, let's replay this scene with Key Three put into practice.

Before you enter the chaotic food fest as lunch monitor, you acknowledge that lunch is a break period for the hard-working students. They deserve to have a free social experience as long as it is safe and kind to others. It is part of balancing schoolwork with a social life, plus it provides nutritional value (questionable for most lunches but still calories). You know from experience that this duty is taxing, but with the proper positive intention you make your move.

You immediately notice the intense wave of noise at high decibels as you move into the active space. It is a wild orchestra of out-of-tune instruments playing all at once, and it is hard to think above the wall of sound. The cafeteria is also a crowded visual collage of color and movement that is hard to navigate, and you are bumped right and left as you move in toward the middle. On your first breath, you inhale a strange mixture of food aromas within the enclosed hall. You have already attended a rowdy school assembly today, so your threshold isn't at its usual handle-anything level. The cafeteria is still a ten on the chaos meter, and you do everything you can to exude a calm and collected nature as you traverse the mayhem. You feel like sweeping the tables clean and blowing a loud whistle to have everyone stop their chatter, but you realize that a lot of the noise is from children's laughter.

The kids are still holding a loud conversation at the center table, and another group rehearses its rap act. Behind the counter, the industrial mixer continues humming loudly. An oven alarm dings and silverware clanks in metal sinks. Then, there's that dropped tray in the lunch line followed by the deafening cheer from the crowd.

You scan the room for anything or anyone who needs attention and spot Carson in the corner. He's not one of your students but you are aware that he is on the spectrum. Carson rocks back and forth next to his aide, making loud unintelligible bleating noises and kicking at the floor. Knees banging under the table, he sends bits of vegetable and gravy and potato flying at the walls. You realize that if you, as the supervising adult in the room, are completely overwhelmed by myriad stimuli of the cafeteria, Carson must be close to a total meltdown. Instead of reacting to Carson's behavior and rushing to stop it, you catch his eye and put your own hands on your ears—motioning that you are aware that it is too loud in here! Then you cross to the noisy center table and huddle with the kids:

You: Hey, you guys all know Carson. He doesn't like loud noises.

The students nod.

You: Look, it's super loud in here right now and Carson is very sensitive, so could you all maybe take it a down a notch?

In a perfect world, every kid in the cafeteria would quiet down. But we know that this may or may not occur. If it does happen— great! Let's imagine that the students lower their voices and continue talking and eating.

Now you are on a roll and you hit up the rap table and repeat the request in a way while complimenting their act. They respond, "Hey, no big deal. It's just a meal." They chill. When the loudest kids take it down a notch, everyone in the lunch room settles down. Even the cafeteria kitchen seems to be much quieter.

You glance back toward Carson to see him calming down. No more kicking. He makes eye contact with his aide and takes a bite of mashed potato.

With peace established, you ask a few other kids if tomorrow they would like to join Carson and his aide for lunch outside if it stops raining. If it is still raining, you suggest that they eat together in an adjoining room to the cafeteria that is private and quiet. From across the rows of tables, Caron's aide gives you a thumbs-up.

This may appear to be a sweet fairy-tale ending. What is more often surprising is how typical kids, if asked to be helpful, are willing to jump to the request. We can learn about our own character only through challenges. They usually bring out the best in all of us.

However, even if the loud students did not calm down, your act of understanding Carson's sensitivities and allying yourself with him can be extremely helpful in the long run. In the future, you may suggest that Carson and some friends eat in a quieter, less chaotic place, such as in the classroom while everyone else is in the cafeteria. Another suggestion might be that he wear head phones or play his iPod when in a crowded area. Ideally, you'd want to hold a sensitivity session in each of the other classrooms so that every student and teacher understands the delicate sensory systems of children with autism.

From the Trenches

Monica Jorgensen, Special Educator

It is so important to see it from the child's point of view. I often stop before entering a room and imagine I am entering a totally unknown environment. I pretend that I have never made this transition and there are unpredictable surprises awaiting me. Then, I put myself in the shoes of a young person with autism. I may be twice as big as he or she is and have many more years of experience to prepare me, and yet I can feel intimidated by new places and faces. I add in the fact that these kids are often challenged to communicate how they feel or what they want. I remind myself that I get frustrated when people don't understand me. I imagine how they feel when they are misunderstood, overlooked, or unable to understand. I notice this helps me build an enduring sense of understanding of their experience.

It only takes me a moment to acknowledge their challenges. When there is a reaction or behavior that seemingly comes out of nowhere, I am aware of the possible influences that may have instigated it.

 Quick Keys

- Remember that children with autism have highly sensitive neurological systems.

- Children with ASD may react abruptly to sensory stimulus and cannot always control their bodies.

- Do your best to filter out harsh environmental elements.

- Experiencing autism from the inside out is the greatest teacher.

Follow the Leader

Discoveries are often made by not following
instructions, by going off the main road, by trying
the untried.

Frank Tyger, *editorial cartoonist, columnist,*
and humorist

When you follow a child's lead, you join him or her in the inner world. This willingness to join children where *they* are becomes a shared experience based on mutual trust and opens the door for the child to join *your* world.

Entering the world of the child with autism requires an open mind. You need to leave behind any expectations about how it should go. This sounds easy but in practice most of us are intent on directing and managing our encounters in all of our relationships. Usually we harbor a preconceived idea, an inner script that dictates how a given exchange should unfold. This is part of our social conditioning and the reason why it may not feel natural at first to truly be led by a child. Being led requires that you resist the impulse to guide or control the child. To work this key effectively, it helps to be genuinely curious about the child's experience. Above all, you will need to allow the child's way of thinking and being no matter what and be open to wherever it may lead. For example, if the child makes flapping motions, don't try to stop him.

73

Go ahead and flap, too. See where this takes you. Odds are you'll be delighted and surprised. Consider this childhood memory of Stephen Shore, who as we've noted has autism yet became a renowned author and international lecturer:

> From a young age, my mother would try to get me to imitate her—but that didn't work. The more she tried, the further I withdrew. Then she tried a whole new tactic—she imitated me. She would flap, spin in circles, and repeat my strange environmental noises. When she did that I couldn't ignore her anymore and, in fact, became aware of her. It stopped me in my tracks. I found someone who was seeing me, hearing me, and on the same plane as me. After we did my thing for a spell, she could pull me into things she wanted to teach me. I would go anywhere with her since she was there for me. The important thing in all educational environments is that before any teaching can occur, the teacher has to develop a positive relationship with the learner. The teacher needs to know that student inside and out.

Because children with autism often process information in ways that are different from typically developing children, they can tend to have narrow interests and it may be a challenge for them to go outside of their comfort zone. We must be willing to be curious about the things that interest them and use these things to create dynamic connections and a genuine relationship. By building on these experiences, you can develop children's ability to socialize; you can expand their range of interests and create rewarding back-and-forth communication. We understand that this can be difficult to do in the constraints of the classroom. But even taking a few minutes a day to see the world from the perspective of the child can create a positive relationship that fosters better learning.

Some people misunderstand this concept and believe that following a child's lead is "spoon-feeding the autism" or allowing inappropriate behaviors to persist. This comes from the assumption that children with autism need guidance and direction at every turn and that it's remiss not to provide it. But that is not the case. As we have mentioned many times, *all* behavior is communication. A child's interests are the best way to learn about her emotional and intellectual life.

The purpose of following a child's lead is not to indulge her but to build trust by meeting her exactly where she is in that moment. For instance, if Susan, one of your six-year-old students, is withdrawn and only wants to stare at her hand, don't attempt to redirect her to something that you regard as more productive. Instead, take a moment to understand this activity. Stare at your own hand. Observe the wonders of the hand: its fingers, nails, palm, veins, and lines. Once you do this, it will be clear that Susan is not disengaged when she stares at her hand but rather she is super-engaged in the amazing architecture of the human hand. When a child sees you sharing her interest, she may look at your hand and you at hers. Suddenly there is an exchange occurring when previously she was alone. You may also notice that Susan is actually able to participate in the classroom better if she is calming herself by gazing at her hand.

After sharing an interest over time, you can expand the interaction based on the child's interests and cognition. Maybe you can put an object in your closed hand and see if she wants to open it up and see what is there. Or you can pretend your hand is a teacup and it is high tea time. You can invite her to join you for tea. From that point, you can discuss the types of tea and if there should be any treats to eat with the tea. Then see if she responds by taking your tea time a step further. Again, ignore the impulse to race through a prewritten script about where all of this might lead. Allow the child's responses to determine the development of interaction. This cultivates the child's sense of self and motivation to connect with others.

> We ought to tend and nourish the internal child, and await his manifestations.
>
> *Maria Montessori*

An excellent method for following a child's lead is the approach created by Stanley Greenspan and Serena Wieder called DIR/Floortime, which directs the adult to literally get down on the floor and experience the world through the child's play. Once engaged with the child, the DIR/Floortime model guides the adult to be "playfully obstructive" to expand the interaction. Being playfully obstructive allows the child to learn to tolerate change and expands the interaction, creating back-and-forth communication. In Dr. Greenspan and Dr. Weider's book, *Engaging Autism* (Da Capo Press, 2006), Floortime is explained as having two goals: one is to follow the lead and preferred interests of the child, the second is to use these interests to help the child move up the developmental ladder and "encourage relating, communication, and thinking."

The first time Neal and Elaine met with Dr. Greenspan, Neal sat on the floor and became fixated on a little doll. Dr. Greenspan coached Elaine to ask Neal for the doll and then take the doll and hide it underneath her t-shirt. Neal had to engage with Elaine to find it. Soon Neal and Elaine became totally absorbed in a game of hide-and-seek. Dr. Greenspan then coached Elaine to offer Neal some crackers to "feed the dollie." Neal took the crackers and pretended to put the crackers in the doll's mouth. This action showed that Neal was capable of advanced thinking and pretend play. It was the first time Elaine and Neal had shared this kind of "typical play" together. Neal's joy in these moments playing with his mom became more interesting to him than just staring at the doll.

When a child with autism retreats from the "normal" busy world into her safe inner sanctum, the typical reaction is to attempt to pull the child out of her isolation. Yet doing the precise opposite can be incredibly effective. If you ask to join the child in her activity, honoring and respecting her needs, she often will be more willing to participate further with you. This, when repeated over time, can relieve her of the fight-or-flight tactics she instinctively employs when she senses that an adult is trying to train her and force her to conform. Let the child lead you on a magical tour of her ingenious inner world and you'll be amazed to discover who that child really is.

When Elaine did Floortime with Neal, and literally sat on the floor with him and experienced the world from his perspective, she found that these times proved to be among the most meaningful and joyous times they had yet shared together.

Floortime enabled Elaine to follow Neal's lead in other situations. For instance, for a time Neal wanted to stop and look at every hubcap when they walked down the street. At first, Elaine pulled and prodded to get him to walk with her. It wasn't easy. Going a block could take hours. But soon after meeting Dr. Greenspan, Elaine took a different approach. When Neal stopped to look at the hubcaps, she leaned down and looked at them with him. There she saw what he was seeing—a beautiful reflection of the sun into the shiny metal of the hubcaps. From that day on, Neal never needed to stop and look at the hubcaps again and they could proceed playfully on their walks.

After Elaine and others connected in Neal's world and created a relationship with him, they began to incorporate "adult-directed" activities, at first for just seconds at a time, then minutes, then hours. The adult would say, "Okay Neal, we will do what you want to do (like swing in a net swing) if you then do something that we want you to do (like learn his ABCs). Before Elaine joined Neal's world, he used to spin in circles, stack match box cars, and could not sit and learn for even a few seconds. Today, he attends a small private home school program where he sits for hours at a time, learning age-appropriate material and sharing his thoughts and ideas through sign language and supportive typing. He has fully entered our world. Joining a child's world is just the beginning of cultivating a relationship with him or her.

In Elaine's early days of working with children with autism, she was asked to work with a nine-year-old boy, Ryan, who pretended to be characters from television shows but could not carry out a typical conversation. His mother thought that an acting class would be good for him, but regular acting classes were too stimulating for him and caused him anxiety leading to meltdowns. She asked if Elaine could work with him privately. In the beginning, Elaine joined Ryan's world by doing with him the only thing he wanted to do: play a toy bowling game. For weeks, they set up the bowling game and bowled for the entire session. Elaine didn't think this was going anywhere and offered to refund the mother's money. But the mother insisted that they keep working together as she said that Ryan enjoyed coming to "bowling" each week.

One day, Ryan brought in a picture book of "The Three Little Pigs." They read it out loud together and then Elaine asked if he would like to pretend to be one of the little pigs. He chose to be the pig that made his house out of straw. From that day on, they acted out the story of "The Three Little Pigs." Then Elaine changed the story to " 'The Three Little Dogs . . . Cats . . . Wolves' even!" She added props and costumes, which Ryan enjoyed. She brought in a typically developing peer who got Ryan to join him in enacting "The Three Little Monkeys." By joining Ryan's world, Elaine opened Ryan's mind to new games, ideas, and ultimately to a new world of fun, imagination, and human interaction.

Following a child's lead doesn't mean just copying what he is doing. It also means being curious and showing a sincere interest in what he is interested in. For instance Henry, who has Asperger's syndrome, happens to love dinosaurs. Among typically developing kids he had always been regarded as weird because he talked about dinosaurs constantly. But in The Miracle Project, we celebrated

Henry's passion for these giant creatures by acting out prehistoric stories, with Henry as our guide. Because of that, Henry became part of a group for the very first time.

A child's interest is the door through which all subjects can be taught. For instance, one year roller coasters became Neal's passion. His week was a long preparation for the weekend at the local amusement part, Magic Mountain, to ride the different roller coasters. It became a recurring activity for months on end. Lisa Johnson, Neal's teacher, used this passion for roller coasters to teach him math, science, simple physics, English, and creative writing. For example, Neal was always concerned that it was going to rain on his roller-coaster day, so they tracked the weather and learned how to read the radar on the Internet. They then explored all the different types of cloud formations as well as weather patterns, high and low fronts, and weather predictions. When they built a model roller coaster, Neal learned about gravity and simple physics. Roller coasters also became metaphors for emotions: anticipation, fear, excitement, and joy. They talked about highs and lows and the uneven track called life.

The child is not the only beneficiary of your joining his world. You will benefit, too, for as you continue to join the child, you'll come to see that his behavior is a form of communication that usually indicates significant needs. Adults who immediately try to extinguish behaviors often miss crucial information. For example, a child may be spitting. To simply address the spitting with "no spitting allowed" and rewarding when she doesn't spit could be a serious mistake. For instance, when Neal started spitting, his pediatrician, Dr. Ricki Robinson, discovered that he had acid reflux and needed medication to support his digestive system.

> It takes one teacher to be creative in his or her exploration of a child to access academic and social development. One teacher can open up the pathway to creative expression of a child with autism.
>
> *Barry Prizant, founder of SCERTS*

The Lock: No Way In

Sometimes the answer you need is literally right in front of you, and if you step a tad to the right or the left, you will get out of your shadow and see the way. In the following scenario, you will meet Sally, who seemed unreachable. Although the outcome of Sally's saga seems improbable, it is, in fact, a true story.

It is already October and you are stumped by a student named Sally, who lives in her own internal world during class. Sally rarely utters a word in class and struggles with social interactions. She tends to keep her head down and avoid eye contact with adults and other kids. She comes to school unkempt: hair uncombed, clothes tussled, and teeth rarely cleaned. On first thought, you assume that she is neglected at home, but she has loving parents. Whenever you talk to Sally, she puts her head down on her desk. You cannot figure out why she is shutting you out. You are warm and friendly and eager for conversation with all your students, but Sally totally ignores you. You're aware that gestures are building blocks of communication that predate the development of speech, so you try using gestures—arm movements and facial expressions—to engage her or at least to get a reaction. Again, Sally ignores you.

At closer range, you see that when she is putting her head down, she is actually looking at celebrity gossip magazines in her lap. She is retreating away from the academics to the vapid news of bitter divorces and quarrelling stars. You are beside yourself. With all the effort to engage her with your lessons, this is what you are competing against . . . and losing. How humiliating.

Sally does not produce any work in the classroom setting. Her in-class assignments are left blank and her homework is a meek attempt to put pencil to paper. You assign a teacher's aide to sit beside her to prompt her through lessons. Sally hangs her head even lower. You try a classmate as a positive peer model, but Sally cowers. You resort to a reward system, but the harder you try, the further Sally retreats. You are at your wit's end and can't hide your disappointment. Sally's team is in the same boat, and even her mom tells you that Sally is intimidated by school in general and by you in particular.

Key Four Exercise: Jump In!

Working with a partner, take turns returning to a state of extreme sensory sensitivity; turn up the volume and intensity on all your senses as you did in the last exercise for Key Three. See if there are any self-regulating movements that can help you regulate the state you're in. These movements could include jumping up and down or staring at your hand or flapping your arms like wings. Once you do any of these activities you'll find that—odd as they may appear to an observer—they are actually coping devices that have the power to calm you. Now, maintain that connection to the movement by continuing to flap, jump, or stare and have your partner react to you in ways that are judgmental, demanding, controlling, and, in general, insensitive to what you're experiencing. "Don't flap you hands. Sit up straight. What are you doing? You have to sit still now." If you don't have a partner, just imagine that someone is saying these things to you.

How does it feel like to have your coping devices interrupted? Let me guess: it doesn't feel good. Try to continue your coping devices while your partner tries to stop you.

Now, engage in the same activities but this time, have your partner tune into (or imagine) your mental and emotional state. Have her be understanding and accepting of your personal coping mechanisms. Then have her join your movements. If you spin in circles, your partner does too. If you flap your arms, your partner flaps. Having someone else share in your calming motions is a new experience that really feels good and creates a special bond between you and your partner.

Notice over the next few days how it feels when friends, family, or colleagues are truly listening to what you have to say and joining your world with interest and enthusiasm. Compare these pleasant experiences to those that come when you feel that things that are important to you are discounted, ignored, or barely tolerated.

The Unlock: Gossip into Literature

After your routine rounds of casual conversation with your students, you ask the withdrawn and uncommunicative Sally about her reading. As you stand before Sally's desk, you notice that she has brought in a stash of fashion and gossip magazines and is secretly reading them. This inspires you to try an experiment.

On the way home from school that day, you stop to buy a few fashion and gossip magazines you know—the ones you would never buy—but love to read in doctor's offices. The next morning, you place the magazines on your desk so that Sally can see them. During silent reading, you casually read one of them. You nonchalantly do this every day for a week. Then one day, before silent reading begins, you ask Sally if she has anything new to read. Sally holds up her magazine and indicates that it has brand-new gossip. You act excited and ask if you can look at it with her. This seems to work out as Sally hungrily agrees. After a few more days, you ask Sally, "Can you believe that Usher broke up with his girl-friend?" "I can't believe it," Sally replies. These are the first words that Sally has ever said to you!

Sally gets excited and tells you even more detailed gossip. Now that her reading acumen and memory are becoming apparent in this verbal exchange, you have a much clearer idea of her level of comprehension. It's a real metamorphosis that was set in motion because you honored her interest without judgment or strings attached. Slowly, you built a comfort zone and a level of trust. By joining Sally, you literally broke through the isolating walls that had entrapped her in her own inner world.

From the Trenches

DanaKae Bonahoom is an internationally recognized leader in the field of early intervention. She specializes in developmental intervention with families of young children, with primary expertise in sensory interaction, communication, and socialization. In addition, DanaKae is the founder of Heartworks Intervention Services.

DanaKae takes the step of "following a child's lead" one step deeper. She calls it "following a child's *need*." DanaKae explains that it is up to the adult—parent, teacher, or therapist—to question why children are doing what they are doing. Ask "what need are they getting from their interest? If children play with cars all the time, see what interests them. Is it the wheels? Kids with autism often love wheels!" she laughs. By going deeper into the need of a child, adults becomes active, engaged, and interested in the *child* even if they are not really interested in the action that the child is doing.

The following is from her weekly blog:

> It is important to take time to LISTEN. Have you ever really listened to your cherub and his/her story?? I ask this seemingly silly question to spur you into deeper and more integral listening patterns. Our cherubs require our "face" to truly listen and hear their needs, loves, desires, worries, hopes, and dreams. They may not always be able to share with true

words, and even when you "hear" them those words may not be "heart" words. This new listening approach will take an act of your will, an investment, and not your brain, or auditory abilities. It's "Face Time"! Once you submit your face to this active listening pattern, you will soon discover that their actions are speaking louder than their true words. All of a sudden, you are struck with the most out-of-sync child, his/her body making movements that in your mind seem painful or meaningless . . . you look more closely . . . and "BEHOLD," you finally HEAR your cherub's communication . . . "Mommy, this world is a very scary place!" In this very moment you question all you are currently doing, yet your child continues moving, you sit still . . . watching this cherub get lost in a pattern that you are not attending to, a communication you are not answering . . . when your faces meet again . . . this time by CHOICE!! You are now connected to his/ her communication, you join the movement, giving smooth movements with a slowing pattern . . . and you two stop . . . a smile beams from the face of your child, and a smile radiates from your heart as you now have just written the newest chapter of your cherub's story; "The Communication Dance!" For those of us who are still trying to etch out some final ink from our old pens . . . here is some GREAT news . . . Within this "new" dance with your child YOU too will be HEARD . . . maybe for the very first time!!!—DK

Quick Keys

- Be curious about a child's inner world.

- Join that world without controlling or trying to force an outcome.

- Expand the play to encourage further communication and then incorporate adult-directed activities.

- Seek guidance from professionals such as your OT or physician when a child exhibits physical behavior or needs that you do not understand.

- Use the child's preferred interests to teach other subjects.

Include the Child

We need to make a paradigm shift. It's not about saying, "isn't it nice that we are inclusive" . . . but about what we can all gain.

Rabbi Mordechai Liebling

Everyone—across all races, cultures, ages, colors, and genders—wants to feel accepted and included. Being part of a community is a basic human need, rooted deep in our tribal instincts. Children with autism are often excluded from the general community due to their perceived "strange" behaviors or social differences.

Many adults and children simply do not know how to relate to a child on the autistic spectrum, so they avoid making contact altogether. This is understandable because it usually comes not from intolerance but from a fear of not knowing "the right thing" to do with a child (or an adult for that matter) who has autism. But, in fact, if one comes with an open heart, curiosity, and from a pure willingness to connect on any level, big or small, you can change a child's world for the better.

Children with autism may appear self-involved, isolated, lacking empathy, and in retreat from the world. Often, this appearance is mistaken for a tacit message that they prefer to be isolated, that they want to be left alone. What appearances cannot reveal is that they often retreat because they have no other way of handling their sensory super-sensitivity. They may retreat because they feel overwhelmed or because they distrust their immediate environment; they may have an instinctive impulse to pull away from things that are unknown, scary, or harsh on their senses; or it may be that after years of being teased and bullied, they come to prefer the sanctity of their own inner world. But the truth is that children with autism are not inherently hermits. They desire friendships and need community like everyone else.

In every Miracle Project class, we debunk the myth that children with autism prefer to be alone. The very same children who, during their school day, may bite, kick, or scream, come to our classes at The Miracle Project and are open, loving, and receptive to one another. They often talk about the importance of friendship and their love and appreciation for their parents and siblings. They share their pain about being bullied, ignored, and misunderstood. When these children are given the space to express themselves without judgment, they convey deep feelings and great insight and are capable of profound human connection.

But the myth persists and when visitors come into our class and see our kids hugging, chasing each other around the room, playing tag, laughing, and sharing their feelings, they often question whether these kids really have autism!

Being part of a community is a
basic human need.

In our experience, these unique children are not only fully aware of what is happening around them but also pick up on the finest details. Even when they appear withdrawn or antisocial, they are oftentimes acutely attuned to the subtleties of a social dynamic. Some children with autism pick up attitudes from the body language of those around them; others sense impatience through vocal intonation; some recognize judgment from facial expressions.

In her book, *Autism Solutions*, Ricki Robinson also challenges this myth that children with autism are incapable of empathy and disinterested in everyday life as the rest of us know it:

> Because children with ASD have difficulty with sensory processing and motor output, their inability to respond or emote the same way we do doesn't necessarily mean they lack empathy. . . . A child with ASD is not detached from life—quite the opposite—he craves everything that life has to offer. It is his sensory process-ing, motor systems, and rhythm and timing issues that seem to derail him from attaining his goal.

So, if you observe a child retreating to his own private island, let him know that he is a valued part of the social circle of the classroom. You can do this by simply mentioning his name and acknowledging that you recognize that he knows what is going on. It is also important to address him just as you would any other child. This conveys to the student (and to the class) that you are not condescending or "baby talking" to him, but treating him as equal to every other child.

Nonverbal children with autism are often the most misunder-stood and excluded. Remember that just because children cannot talk, it does not mean they do not hear or understand. If children don't respond to your request, it doesn't mean they are noncompli-ant. If they don't answer your questions, it doesn't mean they don't understand. If they don't react, it doesn't mean they aren't feeling.

In her book, *Strange Son*, Portia Iverson chronicles her journey with Dov, her severely autistic nonverbal son who appeared totally removed from the world around him. She traveled the world to find someone who could help her reach him. In India, she met Soma Mukhopadhyay, a mother who had raised and taught her severely autistic son, Tito, to write and type. Portia brought Soma and Tito to the United States so others could benefit from her methods. Soma worked with Dov, teaching him to communicate through typing. Once he developed some proficiency, Portia asked him what he had been doing all those years when he was silent. He responded by typing a single word: listening.

> I'm glad you dashed away that pernicious myth that autistic people don't read nonverbal communication. In some ways we may be better at it than non-autistics.
>
> *Stephen Shore*

There are several techniques to foster inclusion and participation among children of all abilities that will not interrupt the general pace and flow of your class. Let's say you ask the class, "Who was the first president of the United States?" A student will raise her hand and say, "George Washington." You can then expand it to include the entire class by saying, "Now, raise your hand if you agree with that answer." In this way everyone, even those who are nonverbal or challenged to speak can participate in an active and timely response.

A similar technique can be used to rate a topic. For example, you can say, "On a scale of 1 to 4, 1 for 'angry,' 4 for 'happy,' rate how you feel about the recent election." Again, all students can rate with a number. This can lead to discussion by the more verbal classmates from which you can form questions for the whole group. You can say, "Raise your hand if you agree with James that you wish more people would have voted." This may create two teams of thinking or unite the classroom with a consensus. Either way, the child with autism will feel part of a group.

You can also give a child with an augmentative communication device enough time to type out his thoughts about a topic while you and the other class members speak about it. Then, you can return to the child who is typing and ask for his response. This way you can keep the dynamic of the classroom active.

When you encourage children with autism to be a valued part of the classroom, you can do so knowing that including them will benefit all of your students. It's a win-win situation that allows typically developing kids to practice acceptance and patience and to learn a lot by being part of a uniquely endowed, diverse community. When you include children with autism, you are demonstrating that everyone is equally valuable, whether they have the same abilities or not.

Elaine's nonverbal son, Neal, became included in the third, fourth, and fifth grades thanks to creative teachers who involved him in all aspects of their programs. In third grade, he participated in the regular education classroom with his aide during art, music, and PE. Neal's third-grade teacher, Ms. Johnson, taught her eight-year-old students about the great painters and had them making their own versions of the painters' masterpieces. Neal loved being part of that classroom and felt proud of and inspired by his "museum" creations.

His fourth-grade experience did not start out in a positive way. He was assigned to a fairly new and inexperienced teacher. She immediately wrote a letter to the principal declaring that she did not want "a boy like that" in her classroom and requested that he be removed. Elaine was furious enough to build a federal case from the teacher's callous remark when fate stepped in and Mr. Sanchegrin or, as he is affectionately known, Mr. S, came to the rescue. When Mr. S learned that Neal was denied admission to the other classroom, he immediately asked the principal to assign Neal to his class. Mr. S is one of those rare and gifted teachers who brings out the best in every student and every situation.

Neal had just started using a choice board to express his wants and needs when he entered Mr. S's class. This simple tool is a dry-erase board with three or four choices written on it that comprise possible answers to a given question. For example, if the class was reading and discussing *Huckleberry Finn* and the teacher asked, "Who was Huck Finn's best friend?" Neal's one-on-one aide would write four choices on the dry-erase board, "Tom Sawyer," "Tom Jones," "Paul Sawyer," and "Someone Else." Neal would then circle or point to an answer.

Mr. S also called on Neal to answer questions in class just like every other student. Let's say he was talking about the Civil War and wanted a student to tell him which president gave the Gettysburg address. He would walk over to Neal and extend each hand with a different answer choice.

"Neal, my right hand is Abraham Lincoln, my left is Ulysses S. Grant. You choose which one." Often Neal got the answer right, pointing the appropriate hand. Mr. S celebrated Neal's achievements and even referred to him as the "resident expert." Other kids realized that even if Neal looked distracted or seemed not to be paying attention, he was actually absorbing the lessons and had a finely tuned memory.

Often students with autism will glance around the room rather than make direct eye contact. Interestingly, many autistic adults express how put on they felt as children when they were being forced to make "eye contact" for the sake of doing so. Michael John Carly, an adult with autism, insists, "Eye contact is overrated."

Mr. S did not demand eye contact because he had enough confidence in Neal and in himself to not need to be looked at directly. He knew that forcing Neal to do so would not only be singling him out but would also derail any genuine communication. Rather, Mr. S totally accepted and respected Neal, which set an example for the entire classroom. In time, the other students came to love and appreciate Neal and wanted to be his friend. They sought him out at lunchtime, played with him at recess, and even made playdates with him after school. Being included in this way made Neal extremely happy and allowed him to make progress at a quicker rate.

In order for Neal to be successful in the mainstream classroom, it was essential that he have a one-on-one aide with him at all times to help him navigate his world and co-regulate his body. This can be costly, but fortunately Neal's school system saw the value in providing this vital support. The one-on-one aide can be a valuable and essential addition to any classroom that includes a child with autism and can also help with unstructured time, such as recess, which can pose added difficulties. If having another paid adult is not fiscally viable in your school district, you might want to enlist the services of a graduate student needing hours or volunteers.

Neal's one-on-one aide, Zack, understood that Neal communicated through gestures, sounds, and pointing at pictures. Zack also became sensitive to the early signs of when Neal needed a sensory break; at such times, he would take him out of the classroom and walk with him. Zack also knew how to include the other kids in games at recess. For example, Neal liked to kick a ball against the wall. He could do this repeatedly, which kept him in his own private world. Zack would bring over the other kids who took turns kicking the ball against the wall with him. Eventually, this turned into Neal kicking a ball to another kid, which then evolved into a real back-and-forth game that was fun for Neal and for the typically developing kids. Zack would also create all kinds of "pretend play" games such as firemen putting out a blazing fire or astronauts going into outer space. These games would expand to include the other kids, and soon there would be a Mars mission under way. The line between Neal and the typically developing students soon began to fade.

Teaching children of all abilities can be a challenge. One of the major obstacles to being included is the inability to readily employ expressive language. Children who have this challenge are apt to need extra time to organize their thoughts and formulate their words. These children often encounter impatience and disregard when they cannot keep up with the usual rhythms of conversation. Yet, as all teachers know, it is essential to validate each and every child, and that begins with allowing them to express themselves, even when those expressions come slowly or are awkward or merely gestural. Patience is a virtue that requires practice. As a teacher, being willing to pause and encourage a response teaches students to do the same.

Eve Mullen, program administrator at C.E.S. (Cooperative Educational Services) in Connecticut, trains her staff to seamlessly include children of all expressive abilities. There can be eight to ten students, some very verbal, others not at all, sitting around a table, each with a different communication device and each one able to get his or her needs met and "voices" heard. There is no interruption in the flow of the lesson.

Wyatt knows firsthand that kids with autism have their own ways of communicating. "A lot of the time, some kids with autism struggle with words or making eye contact," he says, "but they do communicate. I can use words, but I have lots of friends that don't have use of words. But that child definitely has something to say—he uses vibrations. I can even play with them and have a conversation because I can feel their vibrations. We can read human frequencies, which say a lot more than words."

Ido Kedar discovered expressive communication through the use of a letter board at the age of twelve, after a long childhood without any modality to express himself. He presented this "speech" to a conference of special educators:

> Talking is nearly impossible for me. Thinking is not. Talking requires my brain, mouth, and tongue to work together. Thinking does not. Talking is a way to express ideas to others. Thinking is only for myself. Stephen Hawking can't talk but we all know he can think. Lou Gehrig had lost his speech, not his intact soul and mind. The stroke victim has lost his speech but why would he lose his ability to think? I ask this ridiculous question because the reality for some autistic people is that our arms and our mouths don't communicate with our brains, so our output is severely messed

up. Severely messed up is an understatement. Trapped
under sticky goo at the bottom of a pit is more like it.
So, autism is a real prison internally.

It's not a receptive language disorder. Not for me,
and not for lots of others. Can I speak for all? No. But
I do speak for many who sit in class, with intact minds,
watching boring ABC movies and 1+1 math year after
year after year.

There are many ways to include children of all abilities, even
those who are verbally impaired. For instance, you can work toward
a common goal by putting together a puzzle or making a collage.
You can create a story or play that the children can act together.
Creating a daily "drama time" when kids get to act out their
thoughts or feelings and play improvisational games can be fun for
the entire class and can include children of all abilities. Some
children enjoy board games, such as checkers or Monopoly, which
are great for learning to take turns and to follow rules. Others may
enjoy looking things up on Google and sharing information
through the computer. Children who are more physical can participate in simple ball games, races, or follow the leader to help
build relationships with other students. There are many group
activities that can be accomplished equally well with or without
language. Remember, inclusion does not mean plopping children
with special needs at the back of a classroom and carrying on with
the day as if they weren't there. It means making a conscious effort
to include those children in every classroom activity.

For this to work, it will be necessary to accommodate specific
requirements of students with autism and other special needs. They
may need sensory breaks to move and re-regulate their bodies;
they may need special chairs to help them sit more comfortably; they may need curriculum modifications or more time to
complete a given test. Sometimes other students will complain
that it's not fair that some kids get "special treatment." Stephen

Shore, who always wears a hat indoors to combat his extreme sensitivity to fluorescent lighting, has a great comeback to this. He says that "fair" doesn't mean "the same." If one child has to have insulin shots for her diabetes, it doesn't mean that to be fair every child in the classroom should be given a shot of insulin. Similarly, if a child needs a special accommodation for his sensory system to be regulated, it doesn't mean that every student needs the same accommodation.

To help those with severe communication impairments express thoughts and feelings and participate better in school, speech pathologist and augmentative communication specialist Darlene Hanson uses various forms of technology and supportive typing.

The following, typed by a twelve-year-old minimally fluent autistic boy named Dashiell, belies the persistent notions that nonverbals are stupid or devoid of feeling:

> I wish people didn't make fun of me. They don't see me. They only see my disability. If they only knew I am an intelligent man who is saddened by people who tease me. I hope my story will help others understand that autism is not a disease you might catch, but a condition that gives me the ability to see things that others don't.
>
> I can see words in pictures and music in colors. I have the ability to use my sensitivity to understand when a person is hurt emotionally. The only thing that makes me different is that my voice sounds young even though my mind is older. I hope that one day, my voice will match my mind. The only thing that keeps me from understanding others is their ignorance. Sometimes people think that I am not an intelligent person and that I don't have feelings. I can only help myself by learning about my condition. Others should do the same. Together we can . . . make a difference in

building a better society. One of kindness, understanding, and love.

At The Miracle Project we include our nonverbal kids in all class activities by asking them yes or no questions. We give them time to type or write their thoughts and feelings, and we often convert their writings into lyrics for original songs.

Jacob Artson, a nonverbal teenager who types as one form of his communication, wrote the lyrics to our lead song, "Fly":

> If you look long enough. Maybe you'll see why.
>
> Everyone has a talent and they can learn to Fly.
>
> If you look long enough, you can see behind the face.
>
> It doesn't speak but it still feels. Everyone has a place.
> To Fly . . .

Sometimes those with less disability have the most difficulty being included in general education environments. They are often bullied, teased, and called *weird*. But when you delve a little deeper, you'll often find that they have cultivated interests that can enlighten other students. Henry, the boy who loves dinosaurs, can talk for hours about the dawn of civilization; Wyatt spends hours reading about the great spiritual masters; Ezra, who has a photographic memory, knows everything about different species of animals. Include the passions of your special needs students in your classroom! When you appreciate their knowledge, you're appreciating them—and most important, you are showing your other students that these kids are every bit as human and valuable as they are.

Another bogus but persistent myth is that students with disabilities "take away" precious time from typically developing students. A conscious teacher knows the opposite to be true. By including children who experience life differently, you will provide an opportunity for your other students to learn compassion and empathy, to expand their understanding, and to be inspired. The Miracle Project classes include kids of all abilities. Typically developing teens volunteer in our classes for a "reverse mainstreaming." The students with autism learn to model social skills in a natural, organic way. The volunteer teens grow in compassion and understanding. You can create small groups and a buddy system in which a typically developing student can work with a child with ASD in your classroom. Carly, a fifth-grade student at McKinley School in Santa Monica, puts it this way: "I learned more from having Neal in my class than he learned from me. He is so smart. I will never treat a person with a disability the same again."

> We need to give each other space so that we may both give and receive such beautiful things as ideas, openness, dignity, joy, healing, and inclusion.
>
> Max de Pree, American writer, author of
> Leadership Is an Art (Dell, 1989)

The Lock: Top in the Class

When Jordan arrives in class, it is as if a tornado blew in the door as he knocks over a chair and some books fall into an empty seat. His aide Kate picks up in his wake without missing a beat. As you go over to welcome Jordan, he looks like a scared rabbit and he darts across the room to the corner, where he jumps up and down like a twirling pogo stick. Kate finally gets Jordan to sit still in a chair as you start the lesson, but before long, Jordan is back up, another gale-force wind sending him to an empty chair in the back of the room. A flurry of papers dance in his wake as other students look on in amazement.

You ask Jordan a yes or no question but he ignores you and instead releases loud animalistic shrieks. The popular boy in class, Aaron, mimics these animal sounds and the entire class bursts into giggles. He calls it a "Mowgli moment." Jordan races to another desk and spins it around so his back is to the class, sits down, and begins to scribble on a piece of paper pulled from inside the desk. Kate tries to turn him around but you quickly indicate that it's fine for him to stay where he is. Give peace a chance.

Jordan hangs on for a few minutes, but then he springs up, balls up his piece of paper, throws it down, and races to the classroom door. Kate uses her firmest voice as she tells Jordan to stop but he is determined to exit. You let them go as the other students look on. You attempt to resume your lesson plan but you're distracted, wondering if you should follow the whirling dervish or tend to the class. Jordan is your responsibility but so are these other twenty-nine kids. After all, they have already endured so much by this distracting behavior. You will track down Kate after the bell to come up with a strategy for tomorrow.

Key Five Exercise: Stranger in a Strange Land

Imagine that you are at a party in a foreign country. Everyone is speaking a language that you do not understand. They are laughing and enjoying each other's company and completely ignoring you. When you awkwardly try to say something that you learned in that language, people are impatient and condescending toward you. Allow yourself to experience the feelings that come up: isolation, loneliness, and embarrassment.

Now imagine that same party but this time one of the hosts takes it on himself to befriend you. He walks you around the room and introduces you to each of his friends. They show an interest in you and attempt to speak your language. When they don't understand, they take out a piece of paper and ask you to draw what you are trying to say. Together you work through what you are attempting to get across. You are embraced and honored for your differences as the people at the party truly have an interest in including you. How does this feel? Take those feelings in.

Take a day off from talking, writing, or typing and try to get along in the world. See how people treat you. Remember: you cannot write or talk to express your needs, so no one will know why you aren't communicating with them.

When you come to think about it, we are all just one second away from being disabled: a car accident, an illness, or a surgery could leave us impaired. Knowing this, doesn't it make sense for all of us to practice inclusion?

The Unlock: Valuable Contributions

Before the start of school the next day, you meet with Kate, who has been Jordan's one-on-one for two years. She informs you that Jordan has impulsive motor-planning issues and self-regulates by moving and jumping around. Kate suggests they sit in the back to reduce the distractions to you and the other students so they can take movement breaks as needed.

You have another idea. You have a large medicine ball for Jordan to use instead of a chair. He can bounce and move about as needed without leaving his desk, and instead of putting him in the back of the room, you want him to sit in the front. You feel it may give him a stronger sense of community.

After the dramatic exit yesterday, you unballed Jordan's "scribble" paper to find a detailed sketch of a ceiling fan. It was impressive. Jordan had rendered all the working mechanical parts of the fan. This gives you an idea to pair students together to work on a science project.

You ask Aaron to work with Jordan. Aaron's body language clearly states "no way!" but you ignore the protest. Jordan is equally surprised to be paired with the guy who leads the class in making fun of him. Highly agitated, he starts his high jump spin in the distant corner with his excited jungle sounds. You trust that Jordan's mechanical mind will be a good fit with Aaron's propensity for numbers.

You hold up Jordan's sketch of the fan, and assign "Team Jordan-Aaron" to build it using paper, wire, string, and wooden spools. Aaron is actually stunned by Jordan's intricate drawing of the fan, and Jordan gradually slows his body down to listen to this assignment.

Jordan comes to his ball seat and starts drawing the individual parts and variations of how the fan can work. Aaron, now greatly interested, formulates the angles, ratio, and scale of the parts. With sign language and the blueprint, they begin to create their model. They spend the next week designing, constructing, and installing a wind-powered fan based on a pulley system. When Jordan gets an idea, he squeals like a jungle animal and Aaron, too, joins him in the excitement. Jordan is stunned by the advanced math Aaron uses to figure out the mechanics. They submit their final masterpiece in the county science fair, and everyone is impressed as it receives an award for ingenuity. Jordan and Aaron give each other high fives.

Through the process, Aaron sees a different side of Jordan. He likes his unique sense of humor and admires his wide range of interests. He finds out that he and Jordan like the same music and movies. At the same time, Jordan gets to know a more patient, gentler side of Aaron. During free time, they play chess or throw a ball together in the playground. Soon, even Aaron's circle of friends enjoy hanging out with Jordan.

Now, Jordan loves to come to class and sit still on his ball. When he needs a physical break, he and Kate go to the hallway for a few minutes. Aaron sometimes joins him. You are able to pair Jordan with any of the other students who respect his intelligence and contributions and are patient and understanding when he needs his "Mowgli moment." We like to say, "It may take a village to raise a child, but it takes a child with special needs to raise the consciousness of a village."

From the Trenches

Monica Jorgensen, Special Educator

I keep a visual reminder of what appropriate grade-level behavior (both academic and emotional) looks like. It is very easy to have false expectations—either too high or too low—from a child with special needs compared with his or her peers. To keep my perspective tuned in, I create opportunities to combine my special needs class with a mainstream class for reading groups. The students are placed appropriately by reading level. The special needs students have the opportunity to interact with grade-level role models who have the same reading abilities but may have strengths in other areas, such as communication and social skills. I am usually in for an awakening during these peer exchanges. A student whom I believe may have comprehension issues is actually on par with a general education student. Another student I thought had trouble expressing herself is engaged in a debate with a general education student about a certain character in the story. It resets my perceptions about my students' capabilities instantly. The special needs students benefit from this common study group, and their confidence grows when they feel they are on academic common ground with general education students. It is a win-win situation as the general education students also get to experience a teacher who may be more directed and experienced with unique reading challenges. They also have the opportunity to witness the unique points of view from the special needs students. Most important, this exercise puts a new perspective on "appropriate levels" and what expectations are realistic for my own students. When I find that I am caught up in the "how-to-fix" the perceived weakness, I set up this inclusion group and, most often, observe that my students may not be so far off the standard mark and in fact have many gifts to share.

Quick Keys

- Treat children with special needs with respect and kindness. Don't ignore them, talk down to them, or talk about them as if they weren't there.

- Identify the strengths and talents of all children and encourage them to share these abilities in class.

- Offer necessary supports such as one-on-one aides, sensory accommodations, augmentative communication systems, and breaks when needed.

- Use "reverse mainstreaming," pairing typically developing students with children with ASD in small-group activities.

Practice and Preparation Make Progress

Everything is practice.

Pele

If a child is progressing, she is succeeding. It's that simple. This key suggests ways to help a child with autism progress in his own time and in his own way. We enter this process with no expectations, which protects us from frustration and disappointment. Instead, we acknowledge and celebrate whatever microsteps a child takes.

At The Miracle Project, one way that we practice is by establishing routines with which the students can become familiar. For instance, at each session we do movements across the floor. A child may be unable to execute a hop or a skip like other children; however, he is still applauded for his effort. Over time, he may be able to lift his bent knee up toward his shoulder or become more fluid with his arm motions. He may add his own special movement. He may simply have more fun crossing the floor. We keep in mind that progress has many aspects: it can be physical, mental, or emotional. We welcome progress in any of these areas. And we see that each time a child practices, there is an increment of progress, however tiny, that is both significant and a reward in itself

What do children with autism need to practice? Pretty much everything. Tasks such as holding a pencil, brushing hair, or standing in line that are simple to master for typically developing children must be practiced by children with ASD to gain mastery. The many steps involved in new experiences and adventures, such as going on a field trip, participating in a fire drill, or going on the first day to a new school, can be practiced in advance.

As we've mentioned before, many children with autism have difficulty with sequencing and motor planning. When most children see kids chasing other kids around a playground, their brains can compute the activity and they can chose to follow along. But for children with sequencing and motor-planning challenges, simple play can require so many mental steps that it's more agreeable to sit it out. For them, taking part in traditional social games often proves so difficult that they avoid them altogether in order to spare themselves the pain of feeling inept or like a loser. It's not that they don't want to play; it's that they recognize that they can't play at the level of others. So they simply return to their sanctuary, that private, closed-off place that is their safe harbor.

Even the simplest moves such as washing hands, writing names, or using scissors can present enormous challenges. Because basic tasks are so difficult for them to master, people think kids with these challenges can appear "stupid" or "lazy." Often, their families regard them with disappointment or ignore their protests about playing with others or try to bribe them into doing it, which only makes them feel worse about themselves.

Many children with autism have erratic mind-body connections. They may understand what is being asked of them and intend to do it, but their motor planning usurps the intention and does something else. It is as if the body has a mind of its own. This can be incredibly frustrating for the child and is often compounded by an inability to talk about this discrepancy. In his book, *How Can I Talk If My Lips Don't Move?* Tito describes his experience like this:

> I had no problem holding a familiar object in my hands,
> but due to my selective tactile defenses, holding a new
> object was a real pain. Every time I held the pencil, I
> had to focus all of my concentration on the action. My
> senses were strained by practicing holding the pencil,
> resulting in discomfort, the kind you feel when the hair
> on your legs are stroked in the opposite direction of
> their growth. It was like wearing a new pair of shoes.

It is important for you to understand that children with autism are really doing the best that they can even if they don't follow directions or have messy handwriting. They are not being non-compliant or lazy. The key to mastering these activities is to break everything down into small tasks.

Ivar Lovaas, who pioneered ABA (applied behavioral analysis) in the early 1970s, was the first medical practitioner to show that children with autism can learn skills functionally. On the Lovaas Institute website, his techniques call for breaking down skills into manageable pieces and then building on those skills so that a child learns how to learn in the natural environment. Practicing even the smallest pieces of a bigger activity inches the child toward mastery of that activity. ABA, when carried out in a playful, positive way, can be an ideal means to help a child learn functional skills.

Sometimes you must look for other ways to help a child master a task. Perhaps the child has messy handwriting and it looks to you that he gets distracted or is apathetic when it comes to developing pencil skills. He writes outside the lines and takes short cuts, which makes his work illegible. You focus in on the letter A with repetitive exercises on lined paper, but you see little improvement and even diminished results. Both you and the student are frustrated What about practice isn't working here?

What isn't working is your idea of practice. Practice is not about striving for a desired result, in this case, the perfect A.

Practice is about finding the unique paths to progress that suit a particular child and allow him or her to grow. When you hit a wall with a child with autism and progress is elusive, look for other venues in. Seek alternative methods to develop writing skills. Ask your OT for ideas. She may recommend that you not focus on the end result but instead practice drawing big circles on paper taped to the wall just to get the arm and hand coordinated. A terrific website that lists curriculum by Janice Z. Olsen is called *Handwriting Without Tears* www.hwtears.com/hwt and offers age-appropriate products and worksheets to help facilitate handwriting skills. Ultimately, if handwriting still remains too difficult to master, turn your attention to something else such as teaching your student to type on a computer keyboard or talking into a device that turns sounds to printed letters. There is no right or wrong way to progress.

Elaine spent years taking Neal to all sorts of speech therapists—oral motor experts who were determined to get Neal to talk. Neal practiced shaping his mouth, his tongue, his teeth. He blew into whistles to get his breath going—all with little to no success. No matter how hard he practiced—he just wasn't talking. Neal's apraxia, which impedes his ability for his brain and mouth to coordinate, made speaking extremely difficult. Neal's self-esteem was lagging and his desire to communicate was rapidly lessening. Then he met speech pathologist Darlene Hanson, whose motto is "everyone communicates. We just have to listen."

When Darlene introduced Neal to the choice board and to supported typing, Neal's life improved, and his self-esteem soared. Had Elaine only focused on Neal practicing speaking with his mouth, she, Neal, and Neal's teachers would have experienced nothing but failure and disappointment. Instead, she and Neal enjoy the many ways that he expresses himself. Now he practices sign language, typing, writing, and using an iPod touch to communicate.

At The Miracle Project, another way we "practice" is by rehearsing for life's events and challenges. When Jenna started coming to The Miracle Project, she was very nervous about being in a room with other children—mostly because of the sounds. She spent a great deal of class time crying because the room was too loud for her. We chose to help her gain some power over the sounds and had her practice ways to diffuse the sounds when they got too loud.

We had her practice covering her ears to help muffle the sound. We showed her the sign language for *stop* and had her practice using it with our teen volunteers. They would talk, and whenever they got too loud, she could motion *stop* and they would immediately talk more softly. Through these practices, Jenna soon discovered that her needs could be met and this made her far more comfortable in every situation. After successful practices with the volunteers, we then told the class that Jenna does not like it when they get too loud and she will tell us to *stop* or put her hands over her ears when the sounds have gone beyond the point that she can tolerate.

Jenna was overjoyed to find that the very first time she gestured *stop* all of the kids became quiet! It was quite a sight, for these were kids with severe ASD, kids with ADHD, Tourette's, and so on. Yet all of them had compassion and understanding for Jenna. We made a game of this with Jenna as the leader. We'd say *go* and kids would get louder. Jenna would motion *stop* and they would get quiet! Jenna so enjoyed this and, for the very first time, she felt in control of her environment. Soon, she was able to participate in class even when the dynamic grew loud, sometimes putting her hands over her ears, other times motioning *stop*. In time, Jenna became more tolerant of loud environments altogether—eventually singing along with a loud rap track with The Miracle Project Fly Singers and performing for an audience of over twelve hundred people. Clearly, practice made progress.

All the world's a stage.

William Shakespeare

Play-acting and role-playing are also great practice modalities because they engage the children's imagination and allow them to rehearse new situations and try different possible scenarios before participating in them. It gives them a dry run-through of different conversations that may happen, building an internal sense of experience.

In the classroom, if there are projects coming up, give the child some small examples of what is to come. If you are doing a science experiment building volcanoes, introduce the different elements to the child beforehand. Have him feel baking powder and smell the vinegar that will activate the eruption. Introduce the concept of paper mache that will be used to build the cone-shaped mountain. Have him pretend to be an explorer who comes across an island with a live volcano. Use pictures to enhance his imagination. Playful imaginative practice re-creates the activity for the child. The degree to which he feels he has been there and done that is the degree to which he'll be proactive and engaged in the process of learning.

Transitions can cause tremendous anxiety for a child with ASD. It is not the fear of the new place that elicits the fear, but rather what sensory elements that may be *in* that new space that causes alarm. If you introduce a new experience or environment to children in small doses, it prepares their sensory systems and empowers and imprints them with a positive reference. For children with autism, leaving a predictable environment such as a classroom and going into a crowded hallway can feel like going from quiet walk on the beach to entering a tent housing a three-ring circus. The sheer volume of active kids, the close physical nature of crowding, the bright and inconsistent lights, the squeaky loud speaker: it can be a huge insult to their senses.

Stephen Shore, citing his own autism experience, says that the simple task of walking from one building to another can be like walking from Earth to Mars.

> The unexpected elements become exaggerated and even worse, the anxiety factor about what MIGHT be in the new space holds my focus at gunpoint. With a few run-through moments in my mind and even better, to actually experience the new space for a brief moment with a calm and supportive guide, the surprise factor is eliminated and I am able to relax my defenses. I then can see and hear what is actually there instead of the distractions and distortions.

The more a child is prepared with information and practice, the easier the transition will be and the more present the child will be. Visual aids such as photographs of a new space or activity can be very helpful. A picture schedule that shows the day's activities can help ease anxiety of what is going to happen next.

The first day of school can be a big step for children with autism. There are so many new elements to absorb that it can be immediately overwhelming. To prepare for school readiness, encourage parents to inform and arm their child prior to the first day. They can play school at home with a table, chair, and paper with letters and numbers taped to the wall. They can take turns play-acting being a teacher and the new student.

Before Joel returned to school, his mother took photographs of the school that he would be attending—including the school yard, the cafeteria, the teacher, and a few of the aides. She glued these pictures onto construction paper, stapled the papers together, and created "Joel's New School Book." Before the new school year began, she and Joel acted out being the teacher or the student. They even visited the school over the summer. When the school year began, Joel was practiced and prepared to go school.

If the class is planning a field trip to the beach, and you know that the student with ASD has never gone to the beach before, you may want to suggest the following to their parents: Weeks before the field trip, the parents can bring a bucket of sand to the back yard. Have the child feel the sand with his hands and experience it dry and wet. Have the child walk barefoot in a pile of sand and ask how it feels on the soles of his feet. Use a paper cup to make a sand tower. Make the noise of the waves as they crash on the shore. Maybe use a big fan to create wind. Lay out a towel and have a pretend picnic at the beach. This will familiarize the child with the beach elements. Use the Internet to show pictures of different beaches. When it is time for the actual field trip to take place, the child will have had an experience with sand, ocean sounds, wind, water, and most important, will have a positive memory of the beach to draw on. The preparation helps diminish the fear or anxious anticipation.

> Never discourage anyone who continually makes prog-
> ress, no matter how slow.
>
> *Plato*

When situations become unpredictable, unfamiliar, or chaotic, children with autism often retreat to a protective place within themselves. Sometimes this is seen as a complete withdrawal into their own world; at other times it may be revealed as a tantrum.

Activities that typically developing children learn quickly, such as standing in line, making friends, or dealing with a bully, can be confusing for a child with ASD. Educator and consultant Carol Gray developed a concept she calls Social Stories® in which students are helped to regard these things in terms of a story.

By using these stories, you can help your student with ASD feel understood and solve issues that may otherwise hinder his participation. Social stories take an emotion or feeling and put it in a narrative context, removing it from the sensorial experience and putting it into a third-person story. The detachment of the personal allows children to distance themselves form the emotional load of a feeling and see it more objectively. This dovetails into the use of play-acting and role-playing and progresses children to be able to manage sensorial and emotional reactions with a grounded context.

Practice what you know and prepare for what you don't. This is the key for progress!

The Lock: Bridges Falling Down

Here is an example of lack of practice and preparation for an anticipated transition. With awareness, patience, and communication, anxiety and behavioral outbursts can easily be averted.

Fifth grade was great for Olivia. She loved her elementary school where she spent half of her day in the special education annex, a refuge when the mainstream school became overwhelming. She had a special corner beside the bookcase where she would lose herself in her favorite picture books. She loved to look at the architecture of buildings in these books and would spend her recess making her own architectural drawings. Having graduated from that school, she's now moving up to the local middle school for the sixth grade. At her IEP last June, this sounded like fun, but now, in September, she isn't so sure.

Middle school is an enormous, alien city to Olivia. More than two thousand kids are streaming in all directions to different classroom wings through narrow hallways with squeaky locker doors that slam one after the next. The PE fields seem a hundred times the size of the small elementary playground that she knew and loved. She will have different subject teachers instead of a main home-base teacher. It is literally as if she were going to school on Mars.

Her anxiety starts at the drop-off driveway where crowds of kids unload from buses and cars. The kids are all greeting each other with loud shrieks and big hugs. The main gates quickly become blocked by so many kids arriving at the same time. Her mom wants to walk her in, but is forced to move ahead in the carpool lane. The last she sees of Olivia is an image in her rearview mirror of her daughter being swept up into the choppy sea of excited reunions. Olivia clutches her book bag tightly, but a rowdy jock bumps into her, sending her bag flying, her new school supplies falling everywhere. As she tries to grab a rolling pencil case, someone inadvertently steps on her hand and keeps walking. She manages to squirrel out to the side where she sits on a curb until all the students go inside. The piercing school bell rings. She covers her ears and closes her eyes and tried to keep herself from sobbing.

By the time she repacks her trampled supplies and finds her homeroom she is twenty minutes late. She walks into your class-room as you are halfway through explaining the schedule. Her disheveled appearance stops you for an awkward moment, and the entire class is in pause mode to stare at her as she slinks over to the only desk left—in the front, directly under a bright fluorescent light bar. You begin again but the loudspeaker overshadows your voice. The second bell rings, which sends the entire class rushing out the door to first period. Students fling questions at you and when you return to the latecomer, Olivia, she is gone with the flow.

When the bell rings for first period, Olivia walks out into the busy school halls alone. In her panic and disorientation, she can't find any room numbers or the sign for the lavatory. In her frantic search, she bumps into a chatty clique of girls. The lead girl yells at her for being such a dork. Humiliated, Olivia runs away, feeling a warm stream running down her legs. The girls notice and squeal in exaggerated, giggling disgust as they point at her. Their laughter seems to get louder as they disappear down the hall. Olivia throws her books in all directions and rips up her schedule.

By the time you arrive, the situation has gone past the point of no return. Olivia is inconsolable. Her memories of happy school days are forgotten. She hates school and sixth grade and everyone. Including you.

Key Six Exercise: Taking Steps and Let's Role-Play and Pretend!

Place a sheet of paper and a pen in front of you. Take a breath and look at the pen. You are about to write your name, but first stop and think about all of the steps that are needed *before* you do this task.

First, your eyes see the pen. You think about picking up the pen. Your brain tells your arm to move in the direction of the pen. You place your hand on the pen. You direct your fingers to wrap around the pen and so on.

Reflect on how many steps this simple action can take. Imagine if each one of those steps had to be thought out slowly in order to motor plan and execute each time you wanted to pick up a pen and write. Welcome to our students' world.

Imagine doing something for the first time that is outside your comfort zone. It can be something as dramatic as skydiving or as demanding as public speaking, but whatever it is, imagine yourself thrust into the middle of it.

Imagine that you're expected to go immediately to the open door of the airplane where the instructor is pushing you to jump. It is no big deal to the instructor—he does it ten times a day. It's easy for him!

Or imagine that you're suddenly in a bright spotlight and have to address an audience. The crowd is waiting for you. It's no big deal for the speaker who invited you. Just do it!

Now, imagine that you had lessons before skydiving, that you understood the demands and the techniques and trusted your instructor. It may still be risky but you have a clear sense of the ropes. Or imagine that, prior to speaking before an audience, you had visited the stage, spoken into the microphone, and practiced your speech. The spotlight would not be so intimidating.

By practicing, role-playing, and involving the child's imagination, you can turn fears into anticipation and make the unknown a place of exciting exploration.

The Unlock: Building Bridges

Before the end of the school year, you receive an e-mail from a fifth-grade special educator at the feeder elementary school who wants to introduce you to a wonderful student named Olivia. She and Olivia are visiting the school after hours and want to drop by to say hello to meet her new homeroom teacher. You exchange e-mails with the teacher and find out that Olivia has a special interest in architecture and a talent in drawing structures. She finds comfort in this activity and has a special area in a resource room where she sketches buildings.

Before Olivia drops by, you put a Frank Lloyd Wright book out on your desk. At first, Olivia is shy to enter the room, and it takes some friendly coaxing to have her at least peek inside. She scans the room nervously and then spies the picture book on your desk. Like a moth to a flame, she races across the room to peruse it. You show her that you have a special desk in the back corner by the windows reserved for drawing and reading. You have her sit there in the quiet for a few moments with paper and pencil laid out. You invite her to come next week to draw some more. You say you'll bring in a Frank Gehry book. Olivia lights up.

You suggest that the special ed teacher bring her during lunch period, when Olivia can get a sense of the number of kids and general energy of the school. After walking around the active school teaming with loud and rowdy teenagers, Olivia immediately looks for the special drawing corner in her soon-to-be homeroom and takes refuge in the Gehry book. You watch as her anxiety instigated by the din of the school activities fades to a peaceful state as she sketches towers and curvy staircases.

Fast-forward to the first day of school. As you review your attendance, you see that Olivia hasn't arrived yet. The special desk is set up and a collection of architecture books are stacked up on the side. You ask one of the prefects in your homeroom to lead the class through the school protocols before the upcoming first period bell as you slip out to check up on Olivia, clipboard in hand. You find her just outside the school gates, her backpack strewn about and her stare distant. You sit down next to her and start to sketch the school entrance structure: its rounded cupola and iron gate. Slowly, her eyes shift from a blankness to the paper, and as you hand her the pencil, she takes over to fill in the architectural details. Before long, you are both admiring her sketch of this magical gateway to sixth grade. What a beautiful building this is, and there are other annexes to capture with her acute eye and talent. You walk in together as the first period bell rings and the rush of middle-schoolers flood the halls. When you sense her freezing up, clutching her backpack, you suggest that before rushing off to her first class, she come help start the gallery in the back corner. You let her settle at the desk in her comfort zone, now decorated with her first sketch from her first day. Perhaps day two will bring another sketch. You take the time to explain the layout of the school without the other kids in the room and how this resource room is open to her at any time. Olivia has found her foundation in her new school.

From The Miracle Project Trenches

Sloane had long overcome her fears of social groups, but she came to class one evening clearly distressed. She didn't want to participate in any of the class activities and sat by herself holding a stuffed animal that her mom could not pry out of her fingers. Rachel, one of our teen volunteers, sat with her and was able to get Sloane to share that she was scared that there was going to be a fire drill tomorrow at school. We gathered all of the students and volunteers together around Sloane and asked the other students if they had ever been afraid of a fire drill before. Several of the students raised their hands and shared their stories. This instantly calmed Sloane because she did not feel so alone. The students then offered suggestions to Sloane, such as bring earplugs, carry her doll with her, tell her teacher that she is scared, and so on. This not only gave Sloane tools to practice, but it also allowed the other students to feel good about helping another classmate. We then acted out the fire drill and play-acted a real fire! Some kids became the firefighters, some became the burning building, some acted as the fire. The kids all stood in line and waited for the "principal" to motion that the fire was put out and it was safe to return into the school. We discussed how fire drills aren't real and are practice "just in case" of a real fire. We then wrote a song together that Sloane could hum when she got scared. The lyrics included, "It's only pretend, there is no fire. I'm your friend and I'll be right here." Sloane actually enjoyed participating in this "fire drill" and was looking forward to the next day.

The following week Sloane bolted into The Miracle Project all smiles. When someone asked her about the fire drill, she said, "I wasn't scared! I wasn't scared at all!" The kids all cheered!

Quick Keys

- Remember what it feels like to have to think out every move you make.

- Introduce new material and situations in small steps.

- Ease anxiety of transitions by preparing the child for changes with role-playing and social stories.

- When possible use visual aids of unknown places, such as the doctor's office, stores, classrooms, field trips, and so on.

- Engage the imagination and simulate appropriate motor planning through pretend play to create a sense of the new experience.

Key Seven

Live Miracle Minded

The child must know that he is a miracle, that since the beginning of the world there hasn't been, and until the end of the world there will not be, another child like him.

Pablo Casals

One of the most overlooked parts of life is taking time out to acknowledge what is going well, to notice the goodness and progress in a given situation, and to truly connect to a feeling of gratitude and success. Every interaction we have with our students can provide an opportunity to make these heartening assessments.

It is essential to *process* the *process*.

Often we "get through" the day only to be fixated on tomorrow's tasks. Our endless to-do lists can create a vicious, unrewarding cycle that leads to frustration, burnout, and despair. In the case of teachers, for whom the school year is a continual grind, this syndrome is amplified. There always seems to be yet another stack of assignments to read and grade, progress reports to be written, e-mails to be answered, and additional demands from parents and administrators that must be met. We rarely have time to "process the process."

One thing that most teachers, students, and parents share is an appreciation for the concept of "reach for your dreams." Yet we so often fail to notice that many dreams are coming true each and every day. Eckhart Tolle's *The Power of Now* (Namaste Publishing, 1999) explores this concept, pointing out that the only life we live is happening in the moment. Yet, some of us fast-forward to things that have yet to happen or to catastrophes that have yet to unfold, and others are stuck in rewind mode, reliving a past that carries feelings of "would have," "could have," and "should have."

Most of us, to our detriment, vacillate between the two modes. Key Seven unlocks the now in you. It opens you up to live in the present, to see each day anew, each obstacle as an opportunity, and each student as a teacher. Today is a gift. As has been observed, that is why it's called *the present*.

In the now, you teach a child. You connect with that student on a refreshing and exciting level. You follow your educational instincts and watch your students become inspired. You see that your guidance is igniting new ideas and understandings in them.

Key Seven reminds you to enjoy the process, to celebrate victories, however large or small, and, most of all, to stay focused on the positive relationships you are building with your students.

> Happiness is not something ready made. It comes from your own actions.
>
> *His Holiness, the XIV Dalai Lama*

We have been conditioned since youth to be more than what we are right now. This thinking can easily overwhelm any student and is particularly burdensome to a child with autism. Most children with autism are all about the present because they need to use every bit of their focus and energies to deal with and sort out each moment. They are reminders to be in the now, to deal with what is happening right here.

As we've noted before, when you focus on the abilities of each child, you invite them to be seen and heard for exactly who they are—in that precise moment. It's our task to see and hear these children as clearly as possible. Children on the autism spectrum may have extraordinary gifts that tend to go unnoticed. A nonverbal autistic teen using augmentative communication devices can type profound insights about human nature; a ten-year-old who has difficulty with fine motor activities such as writing may be able to discuss complex ideas. A child with ASD may have perfect pitch or acute visual memory. There are countless examples of similar cases.

For instance, this was shown when The Miracle Project's Fly Singers were honored at Carnegie Hall as part of an event called "Genius of Autism." Among the honorees was Stephen Wiltshire, an architectural artist known for his ability to draw an urban landscape to precise scale after seeing it just once from a helicopter. Stephen was sent to a London school where he first expressed his interest in drawing. His passion for drawing was observed and nurtured by his teachers. Neither he nor they had any attachment to a specific goal. In time, his drawings became ever sharper and more sophisticated and his genius was revealed. Today, his work is shown in galleries across the world and carries price tags of thousands of dollars.

Temple Grandin, the world renowned animal scientist, author, speaker, and autism self-advocate, credits her mother and her teachers for seeing the abilities beyond her disabilities. Her science teacher in particular was able to look beyond Temple's emotional outbursts and tantrums and to challenge her to explore her interest in science and her sensitivity to animals.

Even if children with autism are not "savant" or blessed with high-level abilities, they can offer something of value to your classroom. Cynthia's smile is infectious and brightens every one's day. Notice it! Ezra's sense of humor takes the seriousness out of tense situations. Spencer's honesty keeps everyone focused on integrity. It is your opportunity as their teacher to help them realize their potential in the given moment.

The Miracle in the Midst

It's not that I'd written her off, I hadn't . . . but Kayla had just turned four and it had been a year since she'd spoken anything other than "racecar-slippers-blue" and "me-build kang'roo house."

I'd search her quiet, heart-shaped face for a little glimmer, but she'd disappeared. "Where'd you go?" I'd whisper. "Where are you?"

On September 11, 2001, we didn't let her see any news footage. "Take her out of the room," I told Roma, our babysitter, but I know now she must have heard our reactions to the unimaginable . . . all those lives . . . falling in a single moment, heard our whispered pleas of *no!* at the television, the marathon of phone calls we made trying to find people. My office had been on Wall Street.

When my husband and I came downstairs the next morning, Kayla was sitting on the floor surveying her handiwork . . . every wooden block we owned, every Lego, every Tinker Toy . . . arranged . . . in a vast, sprawling cityscape.

Out came the words: "I built you a new New York City . . . with no dead people."

Like the two towers, we toppled. But that's when I knew there was a whole world inside my daughter.

She was still right there.

Miracles happen to those who believe in them.
Bernard Berenson, American art critic

You can see the child with ASD as being difficult, with many challenges, or you can exalt in the moments when you connect with that same child. You can be irritated at the distractions or you can wonder at the gifts he brings to the class and at the way he brings out the best in your other students as they offer compassion and understanding. We have found that when children are seen in a positive light, their disruptive behaviors often diminish and they grow exponentially in ability.

Key Seven invites you to look at teaching as a series of surprises and insights. Both the teacher and the student can be filled with wonder and discovery. The seventh key brings all the keys together in harmony.

Gratitude is not only the greatest of virtues, but the parent of all others.
Cicero, Roman philosopher

At The Miracle Project, it may appear that our unbridled enthusiasm is sometimes over the top. But this one hour each week may be the only time in their school life when these children are seen and appreciated for exactly who they are. It may be the one place in which their deficits are ignored and their gifts are exulted. Use every opportunity to meet each child where he or she is at that moment. If you see that Joey is sad, you can lower your energy. Sit with him and share his sadness. If you meet him where he is, you will talk softly to him and may be able to get close enough to him to figure out what is making him sad. Finally, he tells you that he was bullied at school. You can ask other children if they have ever had this experience and encourage those who have to share their experience with him and with each other. Joey learns that he is not alone, that he is part of a group that understands his experience. His sadness gives way to relief and joy. Before you know it, everyone is high-fiving and happy to be in the friend business. There are myriad ways to build highways to joy at every bend.

You may be the only positive voice that
parent or child hears all day!

One of the most commonly used phrases is "You did it!" It reinforces all good behaviors and expresses your amazement with the child. Any time a child reaches beyond perceived limitations, even by the smallest increment, it's a milestone to be celebrated. Bring on the enthusiasm. The more you wow, the more the child will wow you.

The more parents hear about how well their child did that day, the better they will feel about themselves and their child. You may be the only positive voice that parent or child hears all day! Celebrate the child. Celebrate autism.

The Lock: Color Wars

Jorge is in your seventh-grade class. It's clear that he still has issues getting himself dressed in the morning. Inevitably, he arrives at school with clothes of clashing colors and patterns. Sometimes he wears his shirts and sweaters inside out while the insides of his pants pockets hang out, like a pauper asking for spare change. You often wonder if anyone at home looks him over before he leaves for the day.

Today, Jorge arrives with his mom, Gayle, who is scheduled to attend his IEP this morning. Jorge trips on his loose shoestring and falls on the floor. His laces never stay tied. Gayle is embarrassed and reprimands him. Her frustration builds at Jorge, "How old are you? Tying shoes is mastered in kindergarten. When will you ever get yourself together?"

Jorge's mother then directs her frustration at you. "Can't you see he needs help with organization!! What are you doing about it! Why aren't you helping him where he needs it the most? He doesn't need to know about Greek history or plant categories—he needs to know how to keep himself together!"

Stunned and speechless, you watch Jorge's eyes fade into sadness. Staying put on the floor, he starts rocking back and forth, humming to drown out the yelling. You have seen him do this in the back of the classroom when the class bullies make fun of him. It breaks your heart but the IEP is waiting for you and Gayle. You let Jorge know you will see him during lunch. You wonder how you are going to get through the next two or three hours with a raging mother.

Key Seven Exercise: Minding Miracles, Mining Miracles

Returning to your center, take a couple of deep cleansing breaths. Let your breathing clear away your thoughts and emotions. It may take a few moments to truly find a state of calm inside. Let go of your to-do lists. Let your feelings drift away. You are not suppressing them, just setting them free for the time being.

Allow yourself to be in this moment. Determine what you need on a deep inner level. It may be a pat on the back for a job well done . . . or it may be something as simple as a glass of water. Give yourself what you need. Take time for yourself. Take stock of what you have accomplished.

Using a pen, draw a vertical line in the center of a piece of paper. On one side of the paper list ten major achievements of your life. You might write, I finished college and became a teacher; or I drove cross-country and visited every professional baseball stadium along the way, or I took a risk and left home at eighteen. Once you have finished, go back and on the opposite side of each accomplishment write, "I did it!" Celebrate who you are. Celebrate what you did.

If you are working these steps with a partner, share your list with him or her. One partner will now read the accomplishment and say, "You did it!" You can respond with "I did."

So often we focus on what we didn't do and don't take stock of what we did. Now that you have acknowledged the many achievements in your life, do the same thing for each of your special education students.

On another piece of paper list ten accomplishments that Jorge made this year—no matter how big or small. Jorge lined up with all of the students for the first time. He did it! He wrote his name all by himself! He did it! Jorge and I sat together and shared a story with back and forth communication for over fifteen minutes! We did it!

Let yourself enjoy these moments. These accomplishments are treasures.

The Unlock: A Colorful Rainbow

Jorge is en route to his IEP with his mother when he steps on his loose shoelace and trips outside your classroom. You see Jorge trip and you hurry over to him.

Before Gayle can say more to Jorge than "How old are you!?" you step in front of Jorge to help him up. You silence Gayle by telling her what a special boy her son is. You tell her that he is a breath of fresh air. You say that you can certainly understand how hard it can get as there are so many challenges that she must live with at home. Still, you want her to know that at school Jorge is a treat. You compliment her on the fine way she has raised him. He is a kind and gentle soul with a huge heart. Sure, some days you notice that his clothes don't match, but that is just his personality. When most kids worry so much about their outer garments and make judgments about others based on their outfits,

Jorge doesn't care or see anyone for what they are wearing. It's wonderful, you say, for a budding teenager to be focused on things that are far more meaningful than clothes.

You then show Gayle your Velcro tennis shoes and suggest that perhaps she can find these types of shoes for Jorge so that he doesn't have to always worry about his shoe laces being untied. You also bring in a board with snaps and button holes with buttons that the OT has prepared for Jorge to practice the fine motor challenges of buttoning his clothes. It will take just a little patience and he will be good to go.

Gayle is instantly redirected by hearing about the potential and special qualities of her son. You suggest that you all continue on to the IEP, inviting Jorge to participate. There are many things to review and Jorge's input is valued in his education. Jorge's wry sense of humor has the entire IEP team laughing and upbeat. You see the miracles in Jorge and the smaller but significant miracle of how this meeting took a turn for the best.

Quick Keys

- Allow yourself the luxury of being in the moment.

- Look at what you have accomplished rather than what needs to be done.

- Celebrate all children for who they are and let their parents know their positive contributions to you and to the classroom.

- See the ability within all children and help them to actualize their potential.

- Find the joy in each moment. It's there if you look.

Conclusion
Opening Doors

If you become a teacher, by your pupils you'll be taught.
Oscar Hammerstein, *lyrics from*
"Getting to Know You," The King and I

By now you have read through the seven keys and have at your disposal a whole key ring of suggestions, attitude adjustments, and different ways to view autism. Let's put that new key ring into action and revisit our first closed door.

The Lock: Shut Down

It's the start of a new school year. You've been handed your roster. Jonas Redden is in your class. Your first thoughts are, "What am I going to do? I've seen Jonas through the years. He can't sit down in class; he gets up out of his seat unexpectedly, he spins in circles, and blurts out inappropriate sounds. He goes everywhere with a one-on-one aide and a talking machine."

You tell the principal that you're worried about how a student like Jonas might disrupt the class. You don't mention the fact that you've never received training in working with kids with autism! The principal says you have no choice. Like it or not, Jonas is going to be part of your class.

You wonder, "How can I possibly be successful with Jonas?" You may even feel sorry for yourself and ask, "Why me?"

The Unlock: Wide Open

Key One: First *set an intention* to welcome Jonas. You decide to reframe your fearful thoughts about having Jonas in your class and be open to learning from him. Before you meet Jonas, you take some deep breaths, calm your own system, and become as centered and open as possible. You set an intention to be understanding, patient, and receptive regardless of external influences. Now that you understand the history of autism—what it is and what it is not—you have a framework to begin working with Jonas. You know that every behavior is a form of communication, and you know that you can supply the calm within the storm that will help Jonas feel at peace in your classroom. You see the goals that are set in his IEP, and you are excited to help him realize them. You will do this one day and one goal at a time so that you and Jonas both remain "in the moment."

Key Two: You have already *accepted* your own flaws, your own inadequacies. You know that you and every child in your class are doing the best that you all can. You practice acceptance of Jonas's challenges. You see him for who he is. You accept that Jonas may need to rock back and forth, spin, or get up from his chair several times during class but that he is really listening to the lesson you are giving. You accept that Jonas has a one-on-one aide in class, and you are grateful that his aide can support him when you are with other students.

Key Three: You now understand your own *sensory system* and that the neurological system of children with autism is extremely sensitive. You know that certain sounds, crowds, or too much movement can be overstimulating to Jonas. You seek guidance from the OT to create a sensory diet for Jonas. This "diet" will help him through his school day and also provide sensory breaks, such as leaving the class to run around the track in order to calm his body.

Key Four: You take a few minutes every day to *join* Jonas in his world. You discover that he loves looking at pictures in science books and that he especially loves volcanoes. You share his love of science and bring in your own pictures of volcanoes. You go to the computer with him and Google volcanoes. You use pretend play to act out a volcano erupting. Jonas looks at you and laughs! You connect with him.

Key Five: You *include* Jonas in all class activities. His one-on-one aide, Zev, provides the support that Jonas needs to participate in class, enabling Jonas to answer questions with his iPad, which has voice output. You realize that even though Jonas seems distracted, he is actually paying attention. Whenever possible, you encourage typically developing students to work and play with Jonas. Soon these students are including Jonas without your prompting. Max, an extremely bright and creative student, takes Jonas under his wing and becomes his friend. When a paper is due on friendship, Max writes about how his relationship with Jonas changed his life.

Key Six: As soon as you received your roster, you contacted Jonas's parents and asked them to bring Jonas to your classroom before the school year begins so he could *practice* being in the room and learn where the bathroom and other rooms were located. This practice also includes an opportunity for him to get to know you. You create a picture schedule so that Jonas knows what to expect in his day.

When school begins, if there are changes to the schedule, you let Jonas know in advance and help to prepare him with either stories or pictures. Before an actual fire drill, you have the entire class participate and play-act a fire drill, giving Jonas options to put his hands over his ears if the bells and sirens get too loud. The day of the drill, Jonas does just fine.

Key Seven: You *celebrate* all of the many ways that Jonas has progressed. Jonas is now a beloved member of your class. You have overcome your fears and own inadequacies so that you can appreciate all that "a boy like that" can bring to your classroom. You have opened your mind and your heart. Jonas has become your greatest teacher.

Part Three

Appendixes

The Resource Room
Tools for Using the Seven Keys

Just as most schools have a dedicated room for resources, which can be anything from a quiet sanctuary, a remedial or homework room, a social skills area, a safe lunch spot, or a place to simply share ideas, feelings, and ask questions, we have created this list of resources for you to check into and explore.

As you have experienced, the seven keys focus less on the hardware of a classroom and more about the software of *you*, the educator, and your students. We do hope that the seven keys will invite you to traverse and explore deeper into the vast literature, websites, and information about autism if you so choose. In addition, we will offer you some tangible elements in the classroom environment that can make an impact and complement your use of the seven keys. You will find these in Appendix B, "Additional Corners of the Resource Room," following many of our favorite key-specific websites and resources.

The world of autism is filled with amazing professionals and organizations that offer a wealth of information. Follow your curiosity, interests, and questions using these resources as the doorway in.

Please see our website at www.7keys2unlockautism.com where we will be constantly providing additional resources for you.

Primer: Leading Schools of Thought

ABA: The science of applied behavior analysis focuses on principles (that is, general laws) about how behavior works or how learning takes place. For example, one principle of behavior analysis is positive reinforcement. When a behavior is followed by something that is valued (a "reward"), that behavior is likely to be repeated. Through decades of research, the field of behavior analysis has developed many techniques for increasing useful behaviors. www.abainternational.org and www.lovaas.com

DIR/Floortime: Floortime is a specific therapeutic technique based on the developmental, individual-difference, relationship-based (DIR) model developed in the 1980s by Stanley Greenspan. The premise of Floortime is that an adult can help a child expand his circles of communication by meeting him at his developmental level and building on his strengths. Therapy is often incorporated into play activities on the floor. www.icdl.com

RDI: RDI (relationship development intervention) was developed by Steven Gutstein as a parent-based treatment using dynamic intelligence. The goal of RDI is to improve individuals' long-term quality of life by helping them improve their social skills, adaptability, and self-awareness. www.rdiconnect.com

SCERTS: The SCERTS Model is a research-based educational approach and multidisciplinary framework that directly addresses the core challenges faced by children and persons with ASD and related disabilities and their families. SCERTS focuses on building competence in social communication, emotional regulation, and transactional support as the highest priorities that must be addressed in any program, and is applicable for individuals with a wide range of abilities and ages across home, school, and community settings. www.scerts.com

TEACCH: The long-term goals of the TEACCH (treatment and education of autistic and communication-related handicapped children through the University of North Carolina School of Medicine) approach are skill development and fulfillment of fundamental human needs such as dignity, engagement in productive and personally meaningful activities, and feelings of security, self-efficacy, and self-confidence. To accomplish these goals, TEACCH developed the intervention approach called *structured teaching*. www.teacch.com

Augmentative Communication: Augmentative Communication publishes newsletters and up-to-date articles on augmentative communication. www.augcominc.com

Darlene Hanson: Darlene Hanson is a pioneering speech pathologist whose vision is to provide quality training and support to individuals with severe communication impairments so that their lives are enhanced by communication. www.darlenehanson.com

Autism Organizations

Autism Speaks: Autism Speaks has grown into the nation's largest autism science and advocacy organization, dedicated to funding research into the causes, prevention, treatments, and a cure for autism; increasing awareness of autism spectrum disorders; and advocating for the needs of individuals with autism and their families. www.autismspeaks.org

TACA (Talk About Curing Autism): TACA's goal is to provide education, support, and information to parents to help their children diagnosed with autism be the very best they can be, with the hope of recovery. www.talkaboutcuringautism.org

Autism Society of America: This grassroots group provides a comprehensive resource of protocols and support and exists to improve the lives of all affected by autism. They do this by increasing public awareness about the day-to-day issues faced by people on the spectrum, advocating for appropriate services for individuals across their lifespan, and providing the latest information regarding treatment, education, research, and advocacy. www.autism-society.org

US Autism & Asperger's Association: This organization provides conferences, newsletters, and up-to-date information about autism and Asperger's. www.usautism.org

HollyRod Foundation: Founded by autism advocates Holly Robinson Peete and Rodney Peete, this web community has a very comprehensive resource section for all aspects of autism. www.hollyrod.org/

Stephen Shore: Shore has written several books on autism including his memoir, *Beyond the Wall: Personal Experiences with Autism and Asperger Syndrome*. His website offers valuable information on Asperger's and self-advocacy. www.autismasperger.net/

Temple Grandin: This world-famous animal scientist and autism self-advocate wrote the pioneering book, *Thinking in Pictures and Other Reports from My Life with Autism*, a powerful inside look into the thinking and processing of someone with autism. www.templegrandin.com/

Tito Mukhopadhyay: Mukhopadhyay is nonverbal and communicates his thoughts and feelings through poetry and prose. He has authored several books, including *How Can I Talk If My Lips Don't Move?* which describes his sensory-processing and motor-planning challenges as well as how he perceives the world. His mother, Soma, was his inspirational teacher. www.halo-soma.org

Ido Kedar: Kedar is a brilliant fourteen-year-old nonverbal autistic. Once trapped in an autistic body, he was severely depressed until he learned to type his thoughts and feelings. He now "speaks" at conferences and receives standing ovations for his insight and advocacy for autism. His blog is an inspiration and education into the world of a young man with a severe disability who is nonetheless highly intelligent and communicative. http://idoinautismland .blogspot.com/

Carolann Edscorn: Edscorn was diagnosed as autistic as an adult. In her insightful blog, she shares her thoughts and experiences as she tunnels through the sensory overloads of the world. www.autiecat.blogspot.com/

Chantal Sicile-Kira: Sicile-Kira is an award-winning author, speaker, and leader in the field of adolescence and transition to adulthood. She has been involved with autism spectrum disorders for over twenty years as a parent and a professional on both sides of the Atlantic. Her blog www.chantalsicile-kira .com offers insightful and useful information for parents and educators.

Films

Autism: The Musical: Winner of two Emmy Awards, this HBO documentary stars Elaine Hall, Wyatt Isaacs, Diane Isaacs, and others. Directed by Tricia Regan. www.themiracleproject.com

Dad's in Heaven with Nixon: A documentary by Tom Murray that chronicles his family stories with autism and bipolar issues. www.inheavenmovie.com

Autism Is a World: This Oscar-nominated documentary stars Sue Rubin, a young nonverbal woman with autism, and how she communicates through typing. www.cnn.com/CNN/Programs/ presents/index.autism.world.html.

Normal People Scare Me: Filmmaker Keri Bower's poignant documentary conceived by her fifteen year old son, Taylor Cross, who has autism. www.normalfilms.com/

Wretches and Jabbers: This is a film about two men with autism who embark on a global quest to change attitudes about disability and intelligence. www.wretchesandjabberers.org/about.php

A Mother's Courage: Talking Back to Autism is narrated by Academy Award–winning actress Kate Winslet. This documentary by Fridrik Thor Fridriksson chronicles a mother's journey around the world to find therapies for her severely autistic son. www.amotherscourage.org

Fly Away: A feature film written, directed, and produced by Emmy award–winning producer Janet Grillo about a mother letting go of her severely autistic daughter so that they both can thrive. www.flyawaymovie.com

IDEA and IEP

IDEA: The Individuals with Disabilities Education Act (IDEA) is a law ensuring services to children with disabilities throughout the nation. IDEA governs how states and public agencies provide early intervention, special education, and related services to more than 6.5 million eligible infants, toddlers, children, and youth with disabilities. http://idea.ed.gov

IEP: This site has a long list of questions and answers from a legal point of view about individualized education programs (IEPs). www.wrightslaw.com/info/iep.index.htm

Key One Resources

The Power of Intention by Dr. Wayne Dyer offers inspiring techniques to tap into your personal intentions. www.drwaynedyer.com

Teaching with Intention: Defining Beliefs, Aligning Practice, Taking Action, K–5 by Debbie Miller encourages teachers to align

their core values and beliefs with their classroom teaching. www
.stenhouse.com/shop/pc/viewprd.asp?idProduct=9126

Key Two Resources

Simon Baron-Cohen is a professor of developmental psychopa-
thology and director of the Autism Research Centre (ARC)
at Cambridge University, UK. He is also a Fellow of Trinity
College, Cambridge University. His research into autism spans
three programs: (1) cognitive neuroscience (including genetics);
(2) screening, diagnosis, and epidemiology; and (3) intervention.
He is the author of numerous articles in scientific journals on the
subject of autism and has written several books including
Mindblindness and *The Essential Difference: The Truth About
the Male and Female Brain.* He is also author of a DVD-ROM
entitled *Mind Reading: The Interactive Guide to Human Emotions.*
www.autismresearchcentre.com

Tony Atwood is internationally well known for sharing his
knowledge of Asperger's syndrome. He is a prolific writer, researcher,
and clinician on the subject and works tirelessly with those on the
spectrum, their families, and educators. www.tonyattwood.com.au/

Pema Chödrön is a philosopher based in Buddhist traditions.
Her daily practice of love and compassion is reflected in her many
writings. http://pemachodronfoundation.org

Cheri Huber, a teacher, writer, speaker, and founder of Living
Compassion, is an ongoing resource of self-acceptance. www.cheri-
huber.com/

Alex Plank, Wrong Planet.net was started by a bright and
ambitious teen with Asperger's while he was still in high school
because "he didn't have many friends and had lots of time on his
hands." His online community features blogs, chats, videos, and
articles by, for, and about those with autism. Look for inspiring

articles including one on acceptance by psychologist Robert Nasee. www.wrongplanet.net/article394.html

Laura Shumaker's book *A Regular Guy, Growing with Autism* is a family's story of love and acceptance. www.laurashumaker .com/a-regular-guy-growing-up-with-autism-the-boo

Key Three Resources

How Does Your Engine Run? This book and web community offers an interactive web-based experience to help you understand your own sensory profile. www.alertprogram.com

The Out-of-Sync Child by Carol Stock Kranowitz was one of the first and still most-notable resources on sensory-processing challenges. A must-read for every educator. http://out-of-sync-child.com

Key Four Resources

The Child with Special Needs: Encouraging Intellectual and Emotional Growth by Stanley Greenspan. If you read one and only one book on individual differences and relationship-based interventions, this is it. www.stanleygreenspan.com/books.html

Autism Solutions: How to Create a Healthy and Meaningful Life for Your Child by Ricki Robinson gives parents a greater understanding of their child's unique learning, sensory, and medical profiles. www.amazon.com/Autism-Solutions-Create-Healthy-Meaningful/dp/0373892098

DanaKae Bonahoom and Heartworks identifies the gaps in a child's development, reveals a child's unique sensory profile and deficits, and captures the child's heart and drive by harnessing his or her internal drivers, enabling the child to willingly

climb the developmental ladder. www.heartworksintervention
.com

Key Five Resources

A Place for Me: Including Children with Special Needs provides
tips for making early childhood classrooms inclusive. www.amazon
.com/Place-Me-Including-Children-Education/dp/0935989595

The National Early Childhood Transition Center offers
resources on helping children with special needs transition between
infant and toddler programs to preschool and to higher levels of
school. http://hdi.uky.edu/SF/Home.aspx

Special Education 101, from the Academy for Educational
Development, provides information for parents of children with
special needs including signs that indicate when a child may
need special education services and tips for getting those services.
www.aed.org/News/Stories/speced101.cfm

Social Stories offer a communication technique to put a child's
thoughts, feelings, and emotions within the context of a story.
www.thegraycenter.org/social-stories

Key Six Resources

Vygotsky on Scaffolding: Lev Vygotsky was a Russian psycholo-
gist and founder of cultural-historic psychology. His concept of
scaffolding is explained in *Scaffolding Children's Learning:
Vygotsky and Early Childhood Education* by Adam Winsler and
Laura Beck. www.amazon.com/Scaffolding-Childrens-Learning-
Childhood-Education/dp/0935989684

Mel Levine, *A Mind at a Time*: This world-renowned
pediatrician recognizes each child's intellectual, emotional, and

physical strengths. www.amazon.com/Mind-at-Time-Mel-Levine/dp/0743202236

Rick Lavoie, *The Motivation Breakthrough: 6 Secrets to Turning on the Tuned-out Child:* Tap into the vast written work based on Rick Lavoie's extensive experience working with special needs students. www.ricklavoie.com

Abilitations offers a number of products that help to break down skills and support with unique designs. www.candicelange.com/2006/09/abilitations_special_needs_cat.html

Also check out other product-based sites for educational products:

www.superduperinc.com/
www.linguisystems.com/
www.do2learn.com
www.teachersfirst.com
www.autism4teachers.com

Key Seven Resources

The Power of Now and *A New Earth* are fantastic best-selling reads to connect you to the joy that exists only right here, right now. www.amazon.com/Power-Now-Guide-Spiritual-Enlightenment/dp/1577311523 and www.amazon.com/New-Earth-Awakening-Purpose-Selection/dp/0452289963/ref=sr_1_1?s=books&ie=UTF8&qid=1304774740&sr=1-1

Strange Son by Portia Iverson is about a breakthrough in communication methods for people with autism. Her website offers interactive opportunities for those who communicate through typing to share their thoughts with each other. www.strangeson.com

Following Ezra by writer journalist Tom Fields-Meyer details his developing relationship with his now teenage son, Ezra.

www.amazon.com/Following-Ezra-Father-Learned-Extraordinary/dp/0451234634

Not My Boy! A Dad's Journey with Autism by Rodney Peete is a heartrending, candid look at this NFL superstar's experience, from his son's diagnosis to becoming an advocate with his wife, Holly Robinson Peete. www.hollyrod.org/rodney/not-my-boy

Now I See the Moon: A Mother, a Child, a Miracle by Elaine Hall is a story of faith, hope, and miracles. www.harpercollins.com/books/Now-See-Moon-Elaine-Hall/?isbn=9780061743801

The Anti-Romantic Child: A Story of Unexpected Joy by Priscilla Gilman explores the complexity of our hopes for our children. www.harpercollins/books/Anti-Romantic-Child-Priscilla-Gilman/?isbn=9780061690273

Making Peace with Autism: One Family's Story of Struggle, Discovery, and Unexpected Joy by Susan Senator is a memoir that gives strategies for how to get through the daily issues that autism brings. susansenator.com/makingpeace.html

Mindset: The New Psychology of Success by Carol Dweck explains that teaching a growth mindset creates motivation and productivity. mindsetonline.com/the book/buythebook/index.html

Additional Corners of the Resource Room

E ach year, students spend roughly 5,400 hours at school, most of which are in a classroom. Different types of classrooms have different environments—a sterile science lab has a disciplined, serious environment and the art room has a more creative, playful one. In general, the environment of the main homeroom classes should be welcoming and comforting, one that encourages curiosity without overstimulation. Although the seven keys focus on how you show up in the environment with intention and acceptance, there are certain adjustments that you can make to the physical environment to ensure that each student, and especially a student with autism, has a sense of experiencing the consistent feeling of home in your classroom.

Often a student with autism is unable to sit and focus for long periods of time and may engage in self-regulating behaviors. These reactions may be triggered by a physical element in the classroom that can be controlled or lessened. Sometimes, just being aware of the elements and letting the child know that you understand is a support for a student. It can set up a pattern of co-creating optimal coping mechanisms with the student.

Environmental Factors

Several physical factors should be taken into consideration to create an environment that supports physical, mental, and emotional learning.

Visual

As a general theme, the classroom space should be soothing to the eye without a lot of clutter and competing decorations. Too many posters, hanging objects, busy word-filled walls, bright colors, and cluttered furniture can be overwhelming and distracting for all students and particularly for children with autism. Students tend to feel a sense of being out of control in an overcrowded and over-stimulated space, making it impossible to learn and concentrate. Blues and greens help establish a cooler temperature and are calming, and bright reds and yellows tend to excite. Minimize wall and ceiling art and stick to one theme with a cohesive message, for example, freedom around Martin Luther King Jr. Day, with a poster and a few key phrases from his speeches; or patriotism around President's Day. Scan your room for any overcrowded "hot" spots and use the rule of thumb that less is usually more. The classroom can gradually become more decorated with the students' works, making it their own shared nest with their own interior design.

Natural textures also bring a warm feeling to a classroom. Burlap panels or thatched screens are not expensive and can soften hard angles in the class. Plants and greenery are also soothing for students. The use of textured screens can help diffuse and separate parts of the classroom. It may be helpful to create a special corner as a sanctuary for students who need to regroup and self-regulate.

Lighting

Some kids literally feel sick from overhead bright lighting. We have witnessed students running around, hiding under desks, and unable to focus. The most common school lighting is fluorescent, which usually is placed in permanent fixtures. However, it can be reduced by unscrewing half the bulbs, or replacing with nonflo-rescent bulbs. Fabric screens can also help to diffuse the florescent harshness. One teacher we know hung a white parachute across the ceiling, which the students said looked like a soft cloud of light. You can alternatively add fixtures that provide up lighting versus the down lighting of ceiling panels. Of course, use natural lighting from the window source as much as possible because that is most soothing to the student.

Auditory

Often children with autism have trouble filtering out background sounds from conversations. Groups of other students engage in conversations, backpacks are being rustled into, school ducting systems are powered up, projector fans are blowing, and bells and outside noises bleed into the classroom. Obviously, it is unrealistic to remove the many sounds of an active classroom. There is a natural mix of noise generated from up to forty people in a rectangle space. The point is not to stop noises and have a silent classroom. That is not the way of the world, and it is important to prepare a child with autism to be able to manage himself in the world with all the natural audio input that is occurring at any given moment. Nevertheless, you can be sensitive to the needs of a student with autism by controlling escalating noise levels of the student din. At The Miracle Project, we count backwards with fingers high in the air, 3–2–1, where 1 is totally quiet. You can control volume in direct proximity to a student by using textured screens as buffers. The use of soft meditative music can also set up an auditory atmosphere at the start of class and during transitions.

Classroom Set-Up

The classroom set-up establishes not only the physical structure of each specific learning community but also the routine format. Certain visual supports can be positioned to aid student transition with a sense of reliable and consistent information. Classrooms should be specifically designed to foster optimal learning, and that may mean breaking away from any preconceived traditions of typical classrooms.

Seating

Classroom desk set-up is a contributing factor to the environment you choose to create in the classroom. Some classrooms have strict rows of desks with assigned seats by last name or some other criteria. Row seating can often create a feeling of isolation even in close proximity to others because students are forced to look at the back of other students' heads. Instead of the traditional grid, cooperative group seating, such as desk pods or circles, can foster team building, participation, eye contact, and interpersonal relationships. It is more conducive to creating a sense of inclusion for all the students. When desks are configured together, floor space is kept open for group activities. Sometimes, putting children with autism in the front row can help to keep them engaged more in the lesson; for others, it can be overwhelming. Again, the rule of thumb is to adjust according to what works best for the individual child.

Visual Schedules

Children with autism truly benefit from a clearly communicated daily routine. Visible time lines with tangible parts are powerful aids for students who struggle with sequencing or auditory processing or need reassurance they are on the right track. Schedules can use colors and pictures to assist students with visual discrimination. Some students may benefit from a personal schedule on their desk to assist them with staying connected to the classroom activities as well as their specific additions, such as pull-out therapies. Tangibles help students who have challenges in articulating their needs independently to organize both the external and internal states.

It is helpful to involve the student in preparing the schedule with moveable parts. When changes come up, it is empowering for the student to physically make the change on the visual schedule. It allows the student with autism to visualize the change and prepare mentally for smoother transitions. You will find that typical kids in class also respond to common organizational tools.

Procedures

Clear expectations of the classroom procedures can be calming to children with autism. They often like to know the what, when, and how of tasks that are expected to be completed. Consistent procedures with visual and auditory reminders inform the student about basic things such as how to enter the classroom, listen to lessons, work in small groups, go to the bathroom, sharpen a pencil, answer a question, and so on.

Proactive Tools

Here are a few effective guidelines to help when mainstreaming children with special needs in regular education or in special day classrooms. Use the ones suited to your unique situation; others may not work as well. In any case, these ideas provide nothing less than a fascinating journey.

1. *Honor interests.* Discover and focus on children's interests, incorporating them into a broad spectrum of activities. For instance, if they are passionate about dinosaurs, such as Henry was in the film *Autism: The Musical*, let them lead a class discussion on dinosaurs and prehistoric times. Dinosaurs can also be part of math or science and Henry can be donned the "dino expert." Individual acknowledgment empowers students and gives them a feeling of being important in the group.

2. *Glee club and so on.* Encourage the child with autism to participate in extracurricular classes. If a child loves to sing,

send him in the direction of choir. If she is athletic, sports and PE activities are a great equalizer. The child's strengths will foster relationships with other kids with the same strengths.

3. *Visual tools.* Picture boards and visual schedules can make communication seamless and stress free for children who struggle with verbalizing. They can instantly make the child feel capable of keeping up with the other students by simply pointing to a drawing of a toilet to say, "I need to go to the bathroom." A picture of a tree can mean, "I want to go outside." And a picture of a track can say, "I need to take a walk or run." The child feels empowered to be able to get across a need, such as "I need a break," without words.

4. *Boundaries.* Children thrive with a clear set of rules. Typically developing students often test boundaries to see how flexible they are and if they are indeed enforced. In our experience, it is essential to spell out the rules in any group dynamic. Most children with autism feel a sense of comfort when given guidelines. Rules should be simple, easy to remember, and practiced with consistency. The obvious rules are the noninjury ones: no hitting, biting, hurting, or harming in any way. Others include how to communicate, raising hands, listening to others, 3–2–1 countdown to silence, and so on. It's helpful to write the rules on a blackboard to make sure that everyone is familiar with them. When children can rely on rules without exceptions, they will have less confusion and anxiety.

If a child with autism is unable to follow a rule, it is best not to reprimand or yell, but rather remind him or her of the existing rules. If the behavior continues, it may be best to have the child leave the group until she is able to self-regulate, not as a punishment but rather as a help. Her desire to be part of the group is most often a strong motivator to practice best behaviors.

5. *Organizers*. Offer children with special needs a picture organizer that shows what will be happening throughout the course of their school day. This way they can prepare themselves and be comforted by having a sense of what will be coming next. Autism is known as a *dis-organization*. Often homework planners and folders are disorganized. It is merely a reflection of an individual's lack of motor controls. Take a few beats before starting a lesson to do a checklist of essential elements needed. In those thirty seconds, children can streamline their desks and be organized physically and mentally.

6. A *big story*. Each moment in our day, each day in our lives is part of a bigger story. We all know and cherish great storytellers—whether it's a camp counselor, a best-selling author, a famous filmmaker, or your best friend. Any story, however compelling, is only as good as the storyteller. The more animated and expressive you are as a teacher, the more you will keep the student's attention, of any student, really, but especially a child with special needs. Stanley Greenspan always encouraged his DIR/Floortime specialists to have "high affect" when working with children with ASD. Scientific studies have shown that entertainment and enjoyment actually change the brain chemistry.

7. *Props*. The use of toys, pictures, and puppets often helps children with autism to participate with others. An inanimate object can often act as a bridge between two students. Play therapists often use puppets to help facilitate play and communication between younger children. If one child has hurt another child's feelings, puppets can reenact the incident with all of the emotions. It is sometimes easier for a

child to understand the emotions of the puppet character than to read it in another child. In a case like this, the puppet can be a bridge to satisfying communication.

8. *Foster two-way communication.* An effective way to instigate communication with children with autism is to ask a few questions each morning when circulating around to pick up homework or walking past a child's desk during an independent working moment. Ask general conversational questions such as, "What did you have for dinner last night?" "Did you watch the game last night?" "Are you enjoying your book?" These little exchanges are ways of letting the child know that you are interested in him and notice each student's particular interest. The answers offer clues that allow you to assess a given student's thought process and expressive-receptive language skills. If a student struggles to answer or does not make sense, don't correct her. You are not trying to teach her conversational English but to be there to listen and interact through these mini one-on-one conversations.

This back-and-forth conversation also gives teachers an opportunity to share a bit about their personal life and values. The student begins to relate to the teacher as a person rather than just an authority. Teachers then can add additional students to make it a community conversation along the same topic, which fosters a social exchange.

Example of a Morning Conversation

TEACHER: Hi, good morning, Joe. What did you have for dinner?

JOE: I don't know.

TEACHER (big expression): You don't know what you had for dinner! Did you eat? You forgot . . . I know you ate something last night. Maybe you had what I had—broccoli and peas.

JOE: Ooooh—gross!

TEACHER: What!? You don't like broccoli and peas?

JOE: No way!

TEACHER: Oh, I love them; I guess I won't offer you any.

JOE: *No* way; I don't like it. I like pizza!

TEACHER: Who else would rather have pizza instead of broccoli and peas?

This casual conversation is the foundation of a relationship between Joe and his teacher. His teacher is not talking to him about school; she is asking about him. In this conversation Joe will remember the awful broccoli and possibly use it to engage the teacher again. These conversations take a couple of minutes and begin the wonderful bedrock on which good instruction is built. The addition of other voices in the conversation also opens the door to meaningful interaction.

Accommodations

It is often necessary to accommodate the specific requirements of your students with autism. They may need sensory breaks to move and re-regulate their bodies; they may need special chairs to help them sit more comfortably; they may need curriculum modifications or a longer time to complete a given test. Sometimes other students will complain that that it's not "fair" that some kids get "special treatment." "Fair" doesn't mean "the same."

All students need developmental support. Each student is an individual learner, and by discovering a student's unique profile, you can empower her to achieve academically following her own learning pathway. Sometimes it may require environmental adjustments with assisted communication technologies, such as keyboards, talking machines, and iPads; additional personnel, such as dedicated teacher's aides or one-on-ones; or adaptive protocols, such as testing accommodations, sensory breaks, and ways to follow a child's lead and inclusion tools.

Frontloading

Special educator Lisa Johnson uses a technique called *frontloading* or preteaching, which allows a student with autism to be more engaged in classroom lessons when given foundational preparations. For example, before teaching fractions, a student could make a pizza out of colored paper in order to visualize its parts. The pizza can be cut with scissors literally in half, then in quarters, then in eighths. This solidifies the concept of fractions in concrete terms for a student.

Equally, before learning about astronomy, a student could explore a picture book about astronomy with his or her parents. These preteaching activities allow students to become more engaged and connected in the class. When a student with autism is allowed time to see the big picture and to internalize the lesson, he or she becomes far more likely to learn and to like learning.

Testing

Testing can be stressful for any student. The natural pressures of tests are often amplified in a child with autism. These students have taken many tests throughout their school years, and many have made them extremely uncomfortable so they may have built-in stress memory triggered even before the test actually begins. To alleviate the pressure of testing, here are a few things that can help:

1. *Environment.* Set up the student to test in a small quiet space, such as a counselor's office, a principal's office, another teacher's room, another classroom with few students, or a psychologist's office. Make sure that the student is introduced to the space before being sent there to test, because not presetting the new environment could invite more discomfort than the test itself. A modified testing setting allows

the student to concentrate on the test without background noise, other students, or other distractions.

2. *Clock*. The ticking clock can be a stress factor and counterproductive to students who do not manage time stress. Relieving time restrictions gives a student the space to think through problems without worrying that he is taking too long on a problem. Arranging for test time before or after class or school removes the element of time from the process.

3. *Bundles*. A successful testing modification is to give the test in parts, which allows the student to focus on one aspect of the material at a time. Students on the spectrum can become overwhelmed with organization skills, so dividing the material into smaller bundles helps them have clarity on a more narrow area of the subject. It also creates natural breaks between tests for reviewing and mentally organizing the next part.

4. *Format*. If students have poor writing skills, the use of oral exams or having an aide write down their answers can accurately "test" the knowledge of the student. If they struggle with memory, home tests or open-book tests support the deductive abilities without relying on memory. Project-based assignments can also reveal that the student has mastered the material.

5. *Preparation*. Pop quizzes rarely go well for students with autism. It is best to give advance warning of upcoming exams and spend a lot of time on review and practice tests to make it as familiar as possible.

Sensory Breaks

Students who are challenged with sensory balancing need to have breaks throughout the day. It can be as quick as a minute or two or a whole period to regain a sense of calm and control. As we see with many children, physical movement can reconnect the mind and body and refresh the learning experience. Some simple moves that diagonally cross the midline of the body, such as right elbow crossing to raised left knee and switching back and forth, or patty-cake, are particularly effective to develop the wiring between the mind and body. Shaking limbs out and doing twisting motions revitalizes the body and can be just the remedy when attention feels scattered or fading. A couple of deep full breaths are also quick and powerful techniques to reestablish awareness and focus.

One-on-One Aides

One-on-one aides are there to be a supportive bridge between you and your student with autism. The aide can help translate the incoming and outgoing information. They are well versed on the particular needs of the student and can make adjustments to factors that may cause reactions. They serve to facilitate optimal communication and provide the student sensory regulation breaks when needed.

The one-on-one aide can be a valuable and essential addition to any classroom that includes a child with autism. Experienced one-on-one aides can do more than help the student they are shadowing. They can be a trusted and informed extra pair of hands and eyes in the classroom. If a lesson is divided up into groups, there is an adult in one of those groups to guide and stimulate further insight.

Be resourceful. Draw on volunteers from the community to assist in your classroom if your school district's budget is limited and cannot bring in additional paid staff. College students who want experience, high school students wanting community service hours, and retirees can all be a great help.

Creating Consistency Across All Environments

This component reaches out to the entire team around the child with autism, including educators, all school personnel, family, and therapists. The team members have to be on the same page and approach the child with consistency and predictability.

Educational supports for teachers are critical. It has been found that a teacher who feels supported has more energy and enthusiasm in her classroom. Support can come in the form of physical tools: visual charts, audiotapes, manipulatives, and other learning props. The one-on-one aide can also bring the child's voice to the class. Adapting the learning environment to accommodate special sensitivities is a form of support: lighting source, window distractions, doors and bells, quiet spaces. The greatest support is to have consistency across environments that work together to make the student feel accepted, cherished, and productive.

Creating a User-Friendly System

For kids with ASD, consistency across the home and school environments is key for reinforcing curriculum and IEP goals. The very same voice and language a teacher gives in class is what the parent needs to be mimicking at home. If the teacher has a point system or lexicon for teaching a particular math word problem, the parent needs to be using those same tools, techniques, and even tone of voice at home to generalize learning across social context.

As teachers, we need to equip parents with the same hooks we work with in class to draw students in and give them something into which to dig their academic teeth. Often when parents get children at the end of the day, they are tired, worn thin, frazzled kids. Children with ASD may have no academic juice left for focused homework tasks after school, or they may need them woven into afternoon activities in a way that has the same clear structure repeatedly confronted during class. This can take the form of flash cards, a word game, or a kinesthetic activity. The main piece is that whatever magnetizes the student back into learning, you need to systemize that practice as part of the everyday after-school routine.

We've found the following useful.

Activities that have a clear and marked beginning. A clapping pattern, a set of words, a single nonverbal cue can let the child know that we're getting down to learning now!

Show that there's meat to your activity and double up on materials. If the teacher is using worksheets in class, use the exact same ones at home. When your student zips through the worksheet, compliment correct answers, and pause to work through the challenging ones. Your child will feel a sense of success and confidence—which is so important to build at the get-go—so that you are not faced with a struggle every time you in engage the student.

Show parents how you structure the lesson. Break it down so that parents can easily see first the set-up, the problem, and variables; the method by which you work through the problem; and the results that can be checked against the set-up for accuracy.

Keep the reward loop creative. If you develop moderately predictable reward loops for the students, there is the risk that they will become satiated, but less so if the reward itself evolves over time. It may serve to get them out of that "stuck" mode when it comes to doing homework.

Study buddies. When kids reach ages nine to twelve, it may be appropriate to help them form small study groups but with no more than four children, if possible. They need to be willing and open to working with one another and to spur each other on. You can have them quiz each other or you can have them start at different parts of the homework so that they mix it up and teach each other.

Teaching via story. This can work if teachers take character actions one step at a time and are supported by visuals. One trick with social stories such as "How I Ride the Bus" is to assist kids in making their own library of custom social stories. Keep sentences simple and core to the activity and take pictures of the child through each step. Have the student compile the book, and every time the student is required to ride the bus, review the social story with the child before going on the bus. Prepping the child for what to expect is key.

Visuals. We can't stress this enough. When at home, parents and caregivers tend to lose the visuals. ASD kids need the charts, pictures, and graphs to help order and make sense of their worlds. Teachers, make sure your parents have copies or templates that they can print to use at home. We shortchange it, but our kids need this extra help. They need double reinforcement to help them keep track of their assignments and remind them how to move through different social situations.

Allow kids to be seekers. Kids are naturally seekers. You can make an exercise into a scavenger hunt with appropriate websites and research resources. There are informational resources for every level of learning and functioning online. You can easily sequence three to five resources into a logical progression to prepare and engage students with a topic, and make it a fun adventure along the way.

Sticker systems. A few years ago, American Girl created the Homework Survival Guide, which included a very useful set of stickers to function as visual reminders in class and at home to bring back to class, bring home, get signed, study, and so on. Again, any visual support can give students with attentional and impulsivity issues the extra edge with their academics.

Technology. How can you put technology to work for your students and their families? Replace that home-school journal with a blog. If the child was having a particularly tough day, give the parents a heads up on the blog. E-mail can have little to no nuance, but if you create a blog especially reflective of the student's interests, you will have a communication vehicle between you and the parents that can function as a living, breathing entity, available at any time, and it's green. Vlogs or video logging takes the blog one step further with video messages. You can also schedule weekly Skype sessions with parents to connect about the child's progress, interests, friendship issues, or incidents. By being face-to-face, you may have the opportunity to better problem solve together in a more collaborative way than if you do so over e-mail or the phone. Remember, you're both working on behalf of the child, so however it's easiest, take that path. Then, teachers, the next time you have to call a parent, you might not hear so much of that defensive tone in their voice.

If you meet resistance to your teaching methods from the child and parent, try doing the following:

- Acknowledge that it all can be overwhelming.

- Be methodical. Make lists, charts, and show parents and students how you will proceed *before* you proceed.

- Frame it as positive. Even if the student has made the same mistake over and over again, tell her she's one step closer to nailing it.

- Spoon-feed the solution in small increments to the parent and child. Go more slowly than you think you need to—even if you're already at a snail's pace. Enjoy the pace. Luxuriate. When do you ever get to go slowly? Aren't you always in a rush? Maybe this can be one moment when you don't rush.

Seven Keys to a Smooth IEP

The IEP is a necessary document for public school students with special needs. Navigating through this thick document can be challenging for all parties and often emotional. The IEP is a group design to organize a plan for the student, which means many opinions and ideas need to synchronize, a process oftentimes easier said than done.

As teachers, we come at autism from so many different directions, perspectives, and backgrounds. Whether you are in an affluent suburban school with a handful of students mainstreamed part of the day or whether you teach in a dedicated ASD class, one of your key allies in the relationship with the child is your relationship with the parent. The seven keys can help inform, strengthen, and grow this relationship in many of the same ways that they do when working with the child.

We recognize that the IEP process inherently sets up competing or even conflicting agendas. Here is what we often see in the complexion of the IEP support team:

As an educator, there's only one of you and, facing total resource constraints, you often feel overwhelmed at how to help this child.

At home, a parent may be struggling with profound behavioral issues that educators don't see after 3 PM.

As the administrator in the room, you have to balance all of the requirements of special needs students in your school and may question whether a parent is dramatizing.

As the advocate, you are fighting for the most appropriate services for this child—services that will connect the dots between the IEP goals and the outcomes. You know the law down to the letter and you are there to call it as you see it.

Without the seven keys, this set-up holds all the makings of a full-scale war—and often here that is what we see.

You are about leave your class midlesson for the IEP meeting. The scene is jam-packed, full of sensory overload. One student is hopping on one leg in a corner, another is refusing to do the next assignment, and still another shouts to be heard above the din. The student, about whom you are meeting, has started to melt down over a transition that was managed too quickly by a brand-new aide and is now screaming and rolling on the ground under a table of sticky art supplies as the aide tries, without success, to deescalate the situation. It's bedlam but you have to go. You leave your senior-most aide in charge, grab the IEP file folder, and back out of the classroom.

Two minutes late already, you speed walk—like a duck, heart racing, taste of dread in your throat—toward a meeting that you have no doubt will be contentious. You think, "If I can just get through it." A distant wail echoes from your classroom. Just keep going.

You enter the IEP meeting. The room is too small. There aren't enough chairs. You grab a folding one from a cabinet. The parent appears exhausted and worn as she takes her seat. She is a single parent. Alone, her arms are crossed in a defensive posture. You mug a quick smile, hoping it won't go so badly. Next to her, on "their" side of the table, shuffling papers, the advocate does not make eye contact. The other therapists and specialists quietly file in as the administrator, still wearing her Bluetooth from driving, perches officiously next to a desktop computer in the far corner, ready to record the meeting.

The room is too warm. Everyone signs in on a single sheet, sliding it nervously around the table from person to person, and the meeting begins. You, the teacher, are up. Your hand trembles ever so slightly as you skim the IEP top sheet for a split second and begin to talk about all the anecdotal progress you have seen the student make since the last IEP. You are getting to a good picture of the student on her better days when the advocate interjects, countering that if so much progress has actually been made, why has the parent been called to school three times in the past two weeks? If the speech therapy progress is so great, why was the child unable to ask anyone on the staff to use the restroom last week? If the OT is truly working, how is it that the student, now age eleven, still can't use a fork at dinner?

Around the table, hackles rise. The OT and the speech therapist stumble over each other trying to defend both their positions at once. The parent observes looking down at the IEP that "the services provided aren't enough to meet any of the goals we always talk about in these meetings. None of the therapy is working." As the teacher, you flash back to the child you just left moments prior—writhing under a table. You search the ceiling for an appropriate response.

The school psychologist counters from across the table that this is simply not an accurate reflection of the child. There is an uncomfortable, protracted pause. The mother shakes her head and says, "How can you tell me it's not an accurate reflection of my child? You've seen her for a half-hour once a week since when . . . starting just a few weeks ago? Do you really think you have an accurate reflection of her progress? You're probably still figuring out where to park. I have records of the calls. I know her needs."

The parent is now in tears. The whole room starts trying to talk at once. In a flat voice, the advocate accuses the team of whitewashing the situation. The administrator, now with her dander up, says, "Hold on a minute. This team has over x years of experience and—." The parent interrupts the administrator and tells her that before she says another word, she'd better remove her Bluetooth device or she will file a complaint with the state. As the teacher, you sit there, trapped, as absolutely nothing is being accomplished. No unmet goals are acknowledged, no new goals are identified, and no hands-on solutions are being proposed. What's worse is that everyone's emotional Richter scale is on ten.

Now, let's replay this scene to reflect everyone's using the keys to become allies.

The Greatest Untapped Resource: The Parent

You are about to leave your class midperiod for the IEP meeting. The scene is still jam-packed, full of sensory mayhem. The student about whom you are meeting is still screaming under the table as the aide tries to deescalate. It's bedlam, but you leave your senior-most aide in charge, grab the IEP file folder, and exit the classroom.

Two minutes late already, you take a moment down the hall to employ Key One: Set an Intention. Recalling for yourself that intentions are not goals, you take several deep breaths to let go of the chaotic classroom moment that has passed. Actually picture it fading like an old photograph. It was one instance. Now you are in a new one. Then, ask yourself the question, "How am I going to show up in this IEP meeting right now?"

What does that intention look like? Is it a calm and tranquil forest? Or are you like a ship with an extremely heavy keel weighing over 25,000 pounds, so that no matter how the waves roll, you self-right and pop back up? Feel that full weight of that keel, if that's what grounds you.

Now, you take it a step further and maybe see yourself entering the meeting, not late and flustered, but smiling and calm—maybe even your hair looks fabulous. See yourself sitting with the whole team, working together, agreeing, commenting on how noise-canceling headphones are such a good idea on fire drill days. Further to that end, also ask yourself, "How I am going to be able to stay in this way regardless of external influences in the meeting?"

In a way, it's not unlike Harry Potter, from the well-known book series, when he finally learns to use the patronus charm to keep the very ghoulish dementors from sucking out his soul and silencing him for all eternity. In the novels, when a dementor descends on Harry, he must draw his wand, point it at the creature and repel it by conjuring in his mind a picture or a sequence of pictures from the happiest moment of his life. By willfully, steadily, intending, and holding these images, Harry successfully drives the deadly, all-silencing monsters away.

When going into the IEP meeting, maybe consider what is your patronus charm? What is happiest moment with this student that you can conjure and hold with conviction throughout the meeting? Was it a funny, shared discovery while the two of you were reading in class? Was it a field trip? If the student is new to you, can you envision a moment to come, teaching this student? One you would like to share in the future? Sometimes, when setting our intention, it helps to get playful and be like Harry, calling on a little magic.

That said, if Harry Potter is not your cup of tea and if you visualized the forest or the ship instead, are you the one tree in that forest that is the most deeply rooted and grounded of all? Can you persist in seeing, knowing, and being that tree, or be the ship self-righting as you go—say if the parent and the administrator come to a moment of conflict during the meeting? The trick is being able to call on, return, and maintain your intention when the waves get rough or the forest suddenly seems dark and mazelike.

Contentious meetings can make this hard, so allow yourself some checks and balances. What is your personal or private signal to yourself in the room during the meeting that you need to reset your intention? Is it a word? Is it a tone of voice or a posture someone adopts? Having a self-cue for keeping or resetting your intention while in the meeting is key to keeping your communication and problem-solving skills on track.

Now, a minute later, with your intention fully visualized and set, you smile and walk toward the IEP meeting—continually reiterating the intention to yourself, however it takes shape, in keeping with the greater idea that you and the team are all about to do something amazing for this student.

You enter the IEP small conference room with everyone huddled around an oval-shaped table. You smile, remark how cozy it is in here, and apologize for the late arrival. Without missing a beat, you make eye contact with the parent and cross to warmly greet her as the other therapists and specialists quietly file in. Asking the parent how she is, you see that she is exhausted and worn out as she takes her seat. A single mom, you also notice the slight tear in the knee of her jeans. On the table, you observe the photo she has brought in of her child. You practice Key Two: Develop Acceptance and Appreciation; you fully accept the parent and her child as you first completely accept yourself. You think to yourself, I had a hole in my stocking yesterday from the car door and no one judged me (too much). Being unconditionally accepting of individual differences starts with you. Ask yourself, "Can I fully accept all of my own foibles and quirks so that I can also honor the differences and gifts this parent and her child may also bring to the table?"

The administrator asks if the meeting can begin, commenting that she is going to listen first and then record notes. The room nods. The parent crosses her arms in slightly a defensive posture. She also has brought an advocate. You ask if you can take the seat next to the parent. She smiles, feeling slightly more at ease, and uncrosses her arms.

The meeting begins as the sign-in sheet is passed around. This is when you can take time to check in with yourself. Is your intention still set? Take a moment to employ Key Three: Understand Sensory Profile and explore your own sensory profile, noting possible overloads within the context of the meeting. Sit slightly back in your chair to observe and receive the energy in the room. If you can truly experience your visceral reaction to the energy in the room, noting the dynamics, you will be attuned to the environment and better able to maintain your intention and grounding.

The administrator nods to you to go ahead and start. Breathe. Then, before going into the progress the student has been making under the current IEP, take a minute to briefly acknowledge the challenges the team and the parent may be currently (or may have been recently) experiencing at home. Cite one example from class or during school to show that, as an educator, you possess a real understanding of what the parent may be experiencing, but then bridge with Key Four: Follow the Leader to clearly and concretely demonstrate how a particular challenge can also be seen as integral to revealing how to better work with the child. Challenges are always accompanied by discovery. Don't leave out the discovery when talking through the less-than-favorable behaviors. There's always something good to be had.

If the parent participates in filling the blanks around stories of the child's interests or modes of coping during stressful situations, follow her lead. Take notes. Parents of children with ASD have some of the most resourceful solutions and insights about their kids. When you make them your ally and say, "That is a great idea and something I'm going to try in the classroom; thank you," you not only level the playing field, but you also make the parent an authentic partner, which can open up an entirely new avenue of working together. By staying willing to explore with the parent and the entire team, you will bring energy to the conversation and motivate the team to learn, to teach each other, and to keep on learning.

Also realize in the meeting that motivated team members want to feel included. Key Five: Include the Child means you readily acknowledge through stories or anecdotes to the parents the child's unique contribution to the classroom dynamic. You also show how teachers or team members use the child's interests and moment-to-moment opportunities to find common ground with the student and foster two-way communication. When we truly pay attention to the student's voice and actions, the student becomes a natural part and participant in the flow of the greater communication. Likewise, when we truly pay attention to each other's speech and action during IEP support team meetings, we decrease the chance that intimidation and defensiveness play a part of the meeting dynamics. Inclusion is not just for the classroom but also applies to IEP support team meetings. As a teacher or support team member, if you notice a parent or other team member feeling intimidated or not participating, there are always opportunities to use the child's interests, curiosity, and hobbies to pose relevant questions that naturally draw a person into the conversation.

When a parent talks about his or her child's interests or passions, you will tend to see the armor drop.

As you move through the meeting toward setting IEP goals, recall that Key Six: Practice and Preparation Make Progress and the need to break larger goals into smaller, achievable milestones are paramount for the student and teacher to experience palpable and genuine success throughout the academic year. Stanislavsky, the legendary acting coach, once said, "You cannot eat a whole turkey in one bite. At the very least, you have to start with a drumstick." Break down the goal into parts and you will have a greater sum. Even if you are working on an annual IEP, prioritize the flow of how you will teach toward a goal, noting all the tasks and setting the rehearsal schedule for real-life situations.

What can be particularly hard on the parents is the thorough questioning of our collective ideas of "perfect" or "normal." It can represent such profound grief. This is where the fight in the dog often surfaces. As parents, we are genetically hardwired within our very musculature with a desire to save our children. So understand that the letting go of expectations may happen by degree with many parents. On the one hand, parents need to know that you comprehend the grief, but on the other, the parent and the teacher need to find ways to work together—through e-mail, home-school journals, or regular talks—to keep their eye on the prize, the child. Additionally, if they can each find and share ways to mark each degree of improvement, no matter how small it may seem—a single on-topic conversation, a moment of eye contact, the tying of one's shoes—and work that into the greater strategy for the child, the educator and the parent will experience more joy whether teaching or parenting. If we can work to let go of some of the more rigid expectations and milestones that are not in tune with the child, parents, teachers, and team members will quickly find that progress is already present—in the present.

IEP meetings can be emotionally and physically draining for the entire team. Recognizing that although we will most likely never solve every issue in a single sit-down session, we can change what we each bring to the table at each meeting. By bringing the seven keys from the classroom to the conference room, as the teacher, you provide a pathway for how parents and educators can truly partner. In many cases, the great teachers and parents are already implementing many of these techniques, but to really know it and apply it takes rehearsal.

Teachers, practice the keys with your parents before the meeting, in the meeting, and after, but also in moments when the stakes aren't particularly high. Next time, instead of making the panicked phone call to the then-panicked parent who would ordinarily go into "rescue that child–I'll come right now!" mode, try pausing and recalling the keys. Having a shorthand for the communication with the parent that enables you to solve an issue or answer a question right then and there without all the drama enables three things: (1) you to teach, (2) the student to learn, and (3) the parent to parent. If you start right in during that first IEP meeting and use the keys to develop a partner-based communication between the support team and the parent, the conference room shifts from a war room (or battlefield) to a miracle mile.

As you are wrapping up the IEP meeting goals, milestones, tasks, dates, resources, and signing off—even if it is a less-than-perfect meeting—take a moment to check in with yourself. You can even close your eyes for a second. Ask yourself, "Is your intention still your intention? Have you drifted away from it?" Reset, if necessary.

Remember, that most likely, for the entire parent-support team relationship, you are the SPOC (single point of contact) back to the parent. That doesn't mean you are a second-in-command Vulcan with an overdeveloped sense of logic and pointy ears. It means you are also the leader of the support team in the parents' eyes and you need to lead by example—which means practicing Key Seven: Live Miracle Minded is probably the most critical throughout your life and relationship with this student and his family. Even in the hardest of moments of the IEP meeting, when you as a teacher need your own time out, you need to consistently approach the parent and the student with a sense of discovery and wonder, and celebrate the small victories. To do this, you need to ask yourself, "What are the miracles we have collectively discovered today? What progress have we noted? Did we celebrate it? If not, can we make even a small plan to do so? What solutions have we happened on and how are we inventively and intuitively putting them into play for this child?"

From weighted cafeteria utensils, to a new recess team, to consistent home-school tools, you need to celebrate it all at a tactical level. And, regardless of the legal, financial, familial, or resource circumstances that inform the IEP, can you, as the teacher, find a single a miracle in this child? Better still, can you close this IEP meeting by going around the table with each team member and the parent finding a single miracle for this child and verbalizing it to the group? It may be tough for the parents to let down the armor, but as the teacher (and the SPOC), if they resist, it is so important to hold the keys and your conviction for this student and say, "It's only one miracle. Just one. I know you see it in her."

Index